. and the
FAMINES

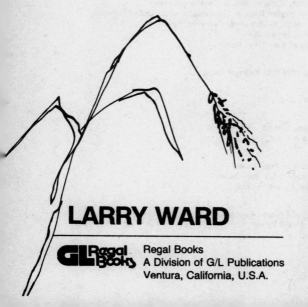

FOOD FOR THE HUNGRY
P. O. BOX E
SCOTTSDALE, ARIZONA   85252
941-0307

LARRY WARD

GL Regal Books

Regal Books
A Division of G/L Publications
Ventura, California, U.S.A.

This book published as part of the information program of Food for the Hungry, Inc., 7729 East Greenway Road, Scottsdale, Arizona 85260

Photos on pages 23 and 71 by Larry Ward

Photos on pages 3, 33, 47, 57, 83, and 93 by United Press International.

Photo on page 105 by World Vision Photo.

The Scripture quotations in *And There Will be Famines* . . . . are from: *The Living Bible*, Copyright © 1971 by Tyndale House Publishers, Wheaton, Illinois. Used by permission. *The New English Bible*, © The Delegates of the Oxford University Press and the Syndics of the Cambridge Press 1961, 1970. Reprinted by permission. Authorized *King James Version*.

Published by Regal Books
A Division of G/L Publications
Ventura, California 93006

Library of Congress Catalog Card No.: 73-82097
ISBN 0-8307-0259-8

In Dedication—
To a Very Special Group of Friends:

The late *Dr. Bob Pierce*, who let his heart be broken by the things which break the heart of God . . . and who taught me time and again in the midst of this world's heartbreak that while we can't do everything, we must do something.

Actress *Tippi Hedren* who leaves the cameras far behind and follows her heart to places like Bangladesh and Haiti and Guatemala . . . who walks through drab refugee camps and dark hospitals in the disaster areas and somehow leaves them brighter through the light of her love.

Dr. Merv Rosell the "Apostle of Encouragement" to so many around the world, and especially to me.

Writer *Dorothy Haskin* and *Mrs. Edith Ross*, who care about others and make friendship a ministry.

Dr. Richardson C. Halverson, who by words and works so often has reminded me that "the most important ability is availability." ("Here am I, Lord, send me.")

C. Davis Weyerhaeuser, Dick Tams, Coleman Perry, Winston Weaver, and *Donald S. Smith,* businessmen who make it their business to demonstrate the love of Christ in tangible terms.

And my Lorraine, whom King Lemeul of Massa must have had in mind long ago when he described a "truly good wife" as one who "sews for the poor, and generously gives to the needy" (Prov. 31:19,20). For over a quarter-century she has shared me with this world's needy. (Right on, O King Lemuel!)

FOOD FOR THE HUNGRY   Signed: Larry Ward
P.O. Box E
Scottsdale, Arizona 85252

Contents

Preface
Let's Begin With A "P.S."

Here in the 1980s I have been tempted—briefly—to toss this book aside and write a totally new one.

But somehow, here in Africa in part of what one newsmagazine calls "the grim famine of 1980," I cannot do that.

I have just re-read this book . . . and somehow my heart tells me to leave it almost exactly as it is. I am merely adding this "P.S." (yes, in the beginning of the book), and then a final "Open Letter" update—convinced that you should feel (yes, *feel*) the deadly progression of the world hunger problem as I have felt it these recent years.

I trust—and hope, and pray—that this will help you more adequately and accurately assess the present precarious position (and future tragedy) of our planet.

In the United States, the *Global 2000 Report to the President* has pointed to environmental, resource and population stresses already severe enough "to deny many millions of people basic needs for food, health, shelter, jobs, or any hope of human betterment."

The Global 2000 Report maintains (and my 22 years of face-to-face confrontation with the world hunger problem only confirms this) that "hundreds of millions of the world's people are trapped in a condition of abject poverty."

And it goes on to project "global problems of alarming proportions by the year 2000."

The situation, I am still sadly convinced, will only get worse before it gets better."

If it gets better.

In my appended update I try to point to some faint-but-hopeful rays of light. But I fear you will only be able to appreciate this little glow of hope after you have worked your way through the darkness of the following chapters.

Admittedly, that's a poor "sales talk" to get you into this book.

But I do hope you will read it.

As I say in the original Introduction, all this has a lot to do with you—with your family, and your future—in the "lean years ahead."

Dakar, Senegal
West Africa

Larry Ward

Foreword

Larry Ward has pushed the panic button this time, and in this most recent of his books makes us feel the hunger of the earth's millions. This is a book about real people whom the writer has seen and talked to, and they are starving.

One thing Larry Ward has done is to quicken the social consciousness of those who have previewed the rough manuscripts, and I'm quite sure you can't read this finished book without coming to a point of significant decision.

In our evangelistic crusades around the world, I have been more exposed to the spiritual hunger of multitudes. I have had the joy of offering them the bread of life. But I have never been completely satisfied when so many of those who so openly received the truth of the Gospel were almost certainly destined for starvation.

We are living in an age of intense specialization. That's why, in my crusade preaching, I must confine myself to the simple presentation of that part of the Bible message which brings life for the endless ages to those people who are certainly about to leave this earth for their eternity. I feel that Larry Ward is also a specialist in this physical part of the world's agony. All that he is doing in this book is to clarify the full implication of the Gospel.

Jesus saw the need of suffering humanity, and He did something about it. He died for sin and for sinners, but He also taught responsibility for those in need. His work was specialized, and He did His work to make possible a new quality of life here and now that would not be inconsistent with our living with Him eternally. There is this continuity of life that begins here and then merges into eternity.

In my study of the Bible and my association with humanity on every continent, I am always aware of the fact that our ministry must be to the whole man. Man is not only "soul," nor is he only "body." With our increasing awareness of the psychosomatic problems, we are made aware of the need that man has as both body and soul. That is why this book is such an important one. There is so much we must say to dying men and women about their souls, but when the stomach is empty and starvation near, they somehow cannot hear our message about Christ and eternity.

The young generation are frequently speaking about being where the action is. I might rephrase this to say that Larry Ward has been where the starving and dying are. That's why, when he writes about it, it comes through to you with tremendous force. You won't be the same when you have finished the book. And if you don't want to be driven to take action regarding the world need, you'd better stay away from this book.

There are also some prophetic implications brought out in this book. It tells about those famines recorded in the Bible such as the one in the times of Joseph as well as the one predicted by one named Agabus in New Testament times. But Jesus included famines with other global catastrophies as signs of the nearing end time (Luke 21:11). There are many things pointing to the consummation of all things and the coming of Jesus to earth again. Famine is just one of them, but it could well be the one that will make its hardest impact. Read this book, and let it awaken your entire being to the imminence of famine throughout the entire world, and the great day of God and the coming of His Son, our crucified and risen Redeemer.

Billy Graham

And one of them . . . stood up . . .
to predict by the Spirit
that a great famine was coming. . . .
Acts 11:28

A Confession

I might as well be honest with you.

This book is written with an ulterior motive.

I suppose anyone skilled in research could write a book on the world hunger problem. The statistics are all right there to be compiled and combined: a burgeoning world, a dwindling food supply, massive technological effort, all the socio-economic-political ramifications.

Yes, I have the statistics, stacks of them, gathered all around the world through many years and millions of miles.

But my statistics have names. And faces.

My eyes still see the deep hurt of their hunger; my ears never quite lose the low moans of their distress.

Vietnam, Nicaragua, Biafra, Bangladesh. These aren't just headlines to me. They spell heartbreak . . . heaped-up heartbreak.

So, I'll be honest. I can't write about world hunger—today's crisis, tomorrow's tragedy—just so you'll be informed. I pray that you'll be concerned, deeply concerned.

And you should be. The same factors which work in our world to create hunger pains in India also cause high prices in Indiana.

For years I have watched the developing world hunger problem and have warned of the crisis to come. Of course I have not been alone in this. There have been respected voices such as Dr. Paul Ehrlich who predicted that "hundreds of millions will die in the famines of the 70s," and the brothers Paddock, distinguished social scientists who took a similar position in their book, *Famine—1975!*

Chances are that many people were ready to view all of us who rang that warning bell as wild-eyed alarmists.

But suddenly, inexorably, the stark reality begins to strike home.

Critical "food-minus" areas have begun to surface; nutritional problems multiply even where food is available; rising concern in the underdeveloped nations is matched by rising prices in the developed.

A newsmagazine strikes a somber chord. Under the heading, "Now a Rising Threat of Widespread Hunger," a feature article declares: "World food production, which appeared healthy and growing only a few months ago, has suddenly shrunk close to the point of global crisis. No mass starvation is reported—but there is widespread hunger."[1]

Surprised? Sound like a new and startling thought? Then remember the words of Jesus, centuries ago. The question was put to Him on the Mount of Olives: "What events will signal your return, and the end of the world?"

In reply the Saviour cited some aspects of "the

beginning of the horrors to come." Perhaps you are familiar with His words: ". . . There will be *famines and earthquakes* in many places."

All this is not just theory. Today it is tragic fact.

The famines are here.

They are going to get worse.

And all this has a lot to do with *you*.

So that's why I have written this book: not only to warn you of the here-and-growing Times of the Famines, but to tell you what all this means to *you* and to *your* family, and what you *can* and *must* do about it.

Larry Ward

1

"What's the First Thing You Think About ...?"

Speak up for the poor and needy. (Proverbs 31:9)

It was one of those typical daytime television interviews; a thing called "Luncheon Date" in Toronto.

TV host Elwood Glover is a pro, smooth and relaxed. He knew better than to sit down with me before the program for a semi-rehearsal—"What shall we talk about?"; "What kind of questions shall I ask you?"— which would make for stiffness and artificiality in the brief dialogue before the camera. So we had chatted just for a moment, to get acquainted. And now the little red light was on and we were on the air. Glover looked into the camera to say:

"Ten months out of the year the man beside me walks through a very different world from the one we know. Today, he's going to tell us about it." And then, turning around to me, he said abruptly, *"What's the first thing you think about when you think about that world?"*

2

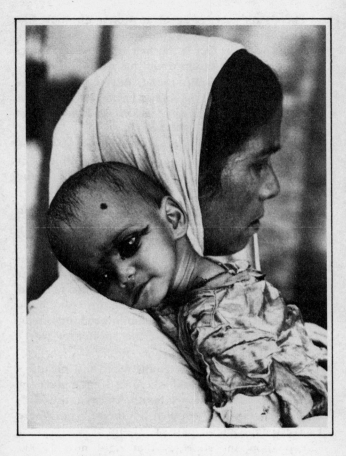

*The plight of women and children
is particularly heartbreaking.*

There's only one way to answer a question like that. It must be answered honestly. All one can do is to tell what in fact *is* the first thing which comes to mind when he thinks about his world.

I thought for a split second, then replied, *"I see an old woman beside the railroad tracks in India. She looks like she is starving to death—and the baby in her arms could already be dead."*

Even as the television interview continued and we talked following this opening about the problems of world hunger, I found myself wondering about the answer I had given.

My service for many years had involved me in many wholesome programs of help to others: child care, medicine, education, technical assistance.

But I realize now (and my answer that day brought it into sharp focus) that in these past years one great burden has emerged like a mountain peak to stand above all the rest. Out of that whole throbbing mass of pain which is the world of human need, one thing haunts me above all others: the specter of world hunger.

I have looked into the gaunt faces and pleading eyes of the starving world wherever I have gone—in Vietnam, Cambodia, Laos, South America, the Middle East, Africa and troubled Southeast Asia, where I have spent a major part of my time.

You know the statistics—that right now 12,000 people starve to death every day, even in this hour of technological research.

But today's crises are as nothing compared to the threats of tomorrow.

4

Today a crisis; tomorrow a tragedy!

Take this already hungry world, where two-thirds of its people are desperately undernourished. But then watch it swell by 8,000 people in the next hour . . . 190,000 in the next twenty-four hours . . . 72 million in the next twelve months.

But those are just figures, and our minds are too accustomed to astronomical statistics. Somehow we all too often fail to translate this truth into the flesh-and-blood reality which it is.

I have felt that reality.

I have held it in my arms.

I cannot forget it.

I see those statistics in terms of that little girl in Laos, her pretty face now like a skeleton . . . as she dies of ordinary dysentery. At last a hot bowl of rice has been placed beside her, but her little body is too weakened from long-term malnutrition. All she can do, as she lies there and dies, is take one little grain of rice at a time and transfer it to the tip of her tongue.

I see the distended tummies and lackluster eyes and flaking skin and loosening hair, a condition men in Nigeria/Biafra learned to call "kwashiorkor," protein deficiency.

I remember how Lloyd Garrison of the *New York Times* described a little boy's death from malnutrition: "He stares at you blankly, without a flicker of recognition. You extend candy, a cup of powdered milk, anything, and the child just stares, too listless, too dehydrated, even to taste. It is the irony of death from malnutrition that in the final fading hours one is at least completely free from the pangs of hunger."

And I am haunted by the words of that man in India. Intelligent, educated, articulate, an adviser to the government of India, he stabbed me suddenly awake, in what had been a previously casual conversation, when he said, "You know, don't you, that we are going to starve to death?"

I looked at him for a moment, at an absolute loss for words. He was obviously serious, yet he had said this in very calm and matter-of-fact tones.

He looked at me steadily, and then continued, "Yes, we are going to starve to death. Every thinking person in the leadership of this country knows that. Oh, we do have some encouragement from 'miracle rice' and what you call the 'green revolution.' But you must remember that we started with a very inadequate food supply. No matter what claims or figures you read, already our food production lags far behind our population increase. And the big problem will come in the years just ahead, when—no matter what is done in the way of birth control—there is just no chance we can keep up."

"We are going to starve to death. . . ." Those words haunted me the next day as I traveled by train deep into the interior of India and saw the inanimate, dry, parched fields, and the human hollow eyes and gaunt faces and pleading hands.

I have been to India many times. I realize that conditions vary from area to area, and that not all governmental leaders share this man's extreme pessimism. But I also know the grim statistics. Says the Population Reference Bureau: "The population of India passed the 555 million mark some time during 1970, according to the best available estimates. It is growing by about 14 million people a year—a rate which will, if sustained, give India a population of a billion by 1990 or 1995."

A billion! Accustomed as we are to astronomical figures, that one should pierce our shell of indifference and lethargy. Another 450 million mouths to feed—another 900 million outstretched hands.

And this is just one country in a world which will reach the 7 billion mark around the turn of the century. Most of that increase will come in the developing nations already confronted with inadequate food supply.

U.S. News & World Report warned on August 20, 1973, that "neither war nor peace, world affairs nor national affairs, count most to most people today. *It's food,* the money to pay for it, and where to get it."

The same periodical added, on August 27 of the same year, that "authorities warn that the whole world—not just this nation—is starting to press against the *outer limits* of earth's resources."

Under the heading, "The Growing Threat of World Famine," Roy L. Prosterman declared in *The Wall Street Journal* (September 14, 1973): "A disaster that could cost as many lives as World War II currently threatens the world. The disaster stems directly and indirectly from the severe food shortage in the less-developed countries."

It may well be that we face again the biblical seven years of relative plenty—and then the most terrible seven years of want our world has ever known.

As William and Paul Paddock put it so succinctly in their *Famine—1975!:* "Today twelve thousand peo-

7

ple died of hunger in the world. Tomorrow another twelve thousand will die. These deaths, however, are nothing more than the warning whistle of the locomotive rushing down the tracks toward the immovable landslide of static food production in the hungry nations. . . . Don't call this pessimism. It is merely sad realism."

A man said, "I have a dream."

I have a dream too.

But mine is a nightmare. A nightmare of pleading eyes and begging hands. The nightmare of world hunger.

That's why I take to heart the words of Proverbs 31:9 in the Bible: "Speak up for the poor and needy."

And that's precisely what I plan to do in the pages which follow.

2

Birthquakes
in Divers Places

And God blessed them and told them,
"Multiply and fill the earth." (Genesis 1:28)

The headlines around the world were beginning to tell the story: India in trouble.

It was late 1972, and I had been traveling across that vast land with my close friend and associate Dulal Borpujari, a distinguished Indian agricultural development specialist.

The "green revolution" was in trouble. Government meetings in India were sparked by heated discussion about the seriousness of the food shortage in many areas. The daily papers were reporting fiery debates: whether or not the situation could in fact be classed as famine; whether or not there were already actual deaths from starvation; and similar sobering questions.

Mr. Borpujari and I were talking with Robert Nave at the famed Nave Technical Institute (named

10

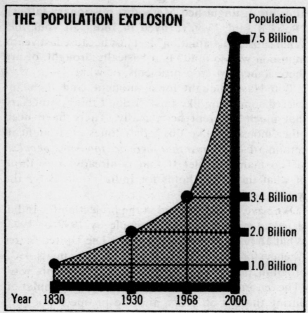

THE POPULATION EXPLOSION

Population
- 7.5 Billion
- 3.4 Billion
- 2.0 Billion
- 1.0 Billion

Year 1830 1930 1968 2000

*One billion equals 1000 million in British usage

POPULATION DISTRIBUTION (In Millions)

	in 1968	in 2000*
U.S.	200	350
Canada, Australia	40	70
Latin America	270	760
Europe	460	570
Africa	330	860
USSR	240	400
India	520	1330
China	730	1480
Japan	100	140
Rest of Asia	590	1550

*Projected figures
Source: United Nations Association National Policy Panel

after his distinguished Methodist missionary father). "Bob," I said, "you've lived in India all your life. What causes this situation? Is it just because last year's monsoon was so mild? Is it basically drought, or are there some new crop problems, or what?"

Bob Nave thought for a moment, and then answered something like this: "I don't think things are that much different here, really. There have been other monsoons like this, other times of drought in certain areas. *It's just that there are too many people.*"

Too many people! If that is already true, think of what the future holds for India . . . and for the world.

We have already looked at the projection for India, slated to swell to a billion people by 1992 or 1993. What about the world as a whole? The United States Agency for International Development, in its 1973 program presentation to Congress, put it this way: "The enormous growth of the world's population during the last 50 years, and the prospects for continued high growth in the future, constitute one of the most formidable challenges confronting mankind."

The report continues: "World population grew to 1.8 billion in 1920, and doubled to 3.6 billion in the fifty years up to 1970. At 1970 growth rates, world population would almost double again to 6.6 billion in thirty years, by the year 2000."

If broad statistics such as these tend to boggle our minds, if we find it difficult to frame a mental image of 6 or 7 billion people, think for a moment about one tiny speck on the world map.

Little Costa Rica has a population of only about

12

2 million. But it is one of the fastest growing countries in the world. Its birth rate is recorded as 45, its death rate at 7 (births and deaths per 1,000 population per year).

At its present rate of growth, Costa Rica will expand in a century to 75 million. That's nearly forty times the present total, and in our world today that would make Costa Rica the eighth most populous nation. But—as Costa Rica grows, meanwhile the rest of the world will burgeon proportionately.

I can almost hear you thinking out loud, "But hasn't all this been said before? Wasn't there this Malthus or somebody who predicted nearly two hundred years ago that the world would soon outgrow its food supply?"

Yes, in his *Essay on the Principle of Population,* published in 1798, Thomas Robert Malthus maintained that while food production increases in arithmetical ratio (1, 2, 3, 4, 5, 6, etc.), population if not restricted grows in *geometrical* ratio (1, 2, 4, 8, 16, 32, etc.). Since both food and the reproductive urge are basic in human existence, Malthus insisted, the world was headed for trouble. True, nearly two full centuries have elapsed since he issued his famous essay (and in so doing sparked considerable controversy).

Was Malthus just the boy who cried "wolf"? (Or perhaps more appropriately, "rabbit"?)

Social scientists today are taking a long and respectful second look at Malthus. Dr. Paul Ehrlich of Stanford University (author of *The Population Bomb* and outspoken exponent of ZPG—"zero population growth") has stated that Malthus was right in

13

his fundamental conclusions, and that only his timing was off.

Answering questions on the complex subject of population growth in the unlikely context of *Playboy* magazine (which, on second thought, is a rather likely forum for this particular discussion), Ehrlich was queried: "Why do you say the death of the world is imminent?"

The distinguished population biologist replied: "Because the human population of the planet is about five times too large, and we're managing to support all these people—at today's level of misery—only by spending our capital, burning our fossil fuels, dispersing our mineral resources and turning our fresh water into salt water."

That was, "at today's level of misery." In the same interview Dr. Ehrlich goes on to point out: "We're adding 70 million people to the world each year. This means we have a new United States—in population and all that implies in environmental stresses—*every three years.* . . . If current growth could continue, in nine hundred years there would be about one hundred people per square yard of the earth's surface."

You of course are thinking something like, "Sure, nine hundred years. But I don't expect to be around quite that long."

No, but in the overall sweep of eternity, nine hundred years really isn't all that long. I have stood in old church buildings of the ancient Mar Thoma Church in the deep south of India and my mind has reeled a bit when it was pointed out to me that these buildings were over a thousand years old.

Perhaps the ancient question of whether or not I am my brother's keeper should be rephrased in this day. As the custodian of this world's dwindling resources, I am my *grandson's keeper* . . . and his world through his adult life will be the incredible one-hundred-percent larger world which to you and me still seems so far removed.

Take a few moments to hear these voices, and see if the reality begins to come home:

U.S. News and World Report: "A new projection by the United Nations shows that, if present trends continue, today's world population will double by the year 2006. The rate of population growth, UN officials find, shows no sign of slowing—and may even speed up in the years ahead."

Father Arthur McCormick, Catholic priest and missionary now teaching at the London Missionary Institute in England: "Actual population increase has tended to conform more to the high than to the low expectation. It is therefore reasonable to project a doubling of world population in this century."[3]

Julian Huxley, former Director General of UNESCO: "The problem of population is the problem of our age. . . . The growth of human population has accelerated from a very slow beginning until it has now become an explosive process."[4]

All of this can seem very dull and dry and academic unless we back up to a basic: *population is people.*

Every one of those seven billion two-legged living mammal units on this crowded planet on January 1, 2004 will be a "people"—a person, a disparate individual.

Perhaps you remember that account in the Bible,

where a woman suffering from a chronic hemorrhage reached out to touch Jesus Christ as He hurried down a road on a mission of mercy.

"If I can just touch His clothing," she told herself, "I will be healed." So she reached out, touched Him, *was* healed, and in so doing prompted a conversation in which Jesus revealed His very remarkable attitude toward people.

When that woman's touch stopped the Lord Jesus Christ, His immediate reaction was, "Who touched Me?"

His disciples looked at Him in surprise. "What do You mean, 'Who touched Me?' You see the multitude—the crowds thronging all around You. They're *all* touching You!"

How wrong they were: "You see the multitude."

They saw the multitude; *He* saw the individual.

Unless God Himself has reached down to replace our calendars with the endless circle of eternity, there will be *7 billion individuals* on Planet Earth in the year 2004.

Not your responsibility? Picture that progression of our children and our children's children as a parade marching toward us down the road of history.

You and I stand beside the shaky bridge of this world's resources. It barely holds the weight of our world at the moment. And it's bound to collapse under theirs. But they're headed this way, and we'd better prepare to do something.

Where do we start? A logical first step is to make sure we see them—both today's needy masses and tomorrow's—as the individuals they are.

I leave to later discussion the sensitive issue of

population control, and the incredible spin-off of realistic concerns which grow out of even very logical and conservative population projections. (For example, take the relationship of population density and social pathology. In an experiment, rats were allowed to increase in population in a confined space. They developed abnormal patterns of behavior which could eventually lead to their extinction.)

We must in a later chapter consider the realistic threat to our world's future posed by the growing hunger crisis. Recent studies of the effects of long-term malnutrition on the brain development of children indicate an eventual threat to entire populations in the overpopulated underdeveloped malnourished areas of the earth.

But let us at this point come back to the basic: our world, whatever its aggregate size, is made up of people who landed on our planet one at a time. *They are individuals.*

I prayed a strange prayer one morning in India. I'm sure I thought I meant it, but I certainly didn't stop to think of all that I was saying as I prayed: "Help me, God, to see the world today with different eyes. Give me," I recklessly went on to pray, "eyes like the eyes of Christ. Help me to see the world around me today as He would see it."

I opened my eyes, stood up—and suddenly it seemed that I did see the world around me as I had never seen it before.

I looked at my watch, and saw time as the gift of God it is: 24 bright-and-sparkling new hours each day—hours we have never lived before in eternity, hours that we shall never live again. Time that we can invest for ourselves, for our pleasure and self-gratification—or time that we can invest for God and for eternity.

I walked the dusty streets that morning, and I saw a beggar with an outstretched hand. But I prayed and looked again with the eyes of Christ, and I saw a brother instead of a beggar and my heart went out to him in love. . . .

A tiny child dashed across my path in the midst of his play, tripped over my feet. I bent down to steady him—this dirty urchin with ragged clothes. But as I looked with the understanding eyes of Christ, he was suddenly my child and your child and above all His child, and I knew then why "Jesus loves the little children, all the children of the world. . . ."

I stood in the teeming marketplace, and looked with those strange new eyes of mine, and suddenly the crowd was gone. There was no crowd now. Just people. *Individuals.* These were men and women, boys and girls, with disparate needs and interests—hearts and homes and hopes and heartaches all their own. And I looked at the multitude and had compassion on them because they were not really a multitude—but a man whose wife had just died, and a woman whose children did not have enough to eat, and a boy who had just failed in school, and a girl who had lost her love. I saw them with these new eyes of mine that were not merely mine, and I loved them with a love that was not merely mine. . . .

I saw the birds on the wing against the azure sky . . . the tropic flowers that bloomed in gay profusion . . . the food placed upon my plate—and all of these, in the divine dimension of my newfound sight, I saw as the tokens of God's love. I saw them as I had never seen them before. . . .

What kind of eyes were they, the eyes He gave me that day?

Ordinary eyes, I guess.

Just like the ones I had had before.

Except for one thing.

These eyes—His eyes—were full of tears.

3

A Six-Letter
Obscenity

*He who shuts his ears to the cries
of the poor will be ignored
in his own time of need. (Proverbs 21:13)*

It's an ugly, six-letter word.

It is, in fact, *a six-letter obscenity.*

Let me give you the background of that statement.

Lenny Bruce, the "sick" comedian, once ventured this acid indictment: "I know in my heart, by pure logic, that any man who claims to be a leader of the Church is a hustler if he has two suits in a world in which most people have none."

In his very remarkable book, *Include Me Out,* Colin Morris reacts to Bruce's statement with these words: "Anyone in the house care to argue? We can comfort ourselves, if we will, with the knowledge that Bruce was banned from every public place of entertainment in the United States for obscenity and died virtually penniless. Does that reinforce our sense of virtue," asks Morris, "or can we see that what he was describing is a far greater obscenity than all the filth that poured from his mouth?"

22

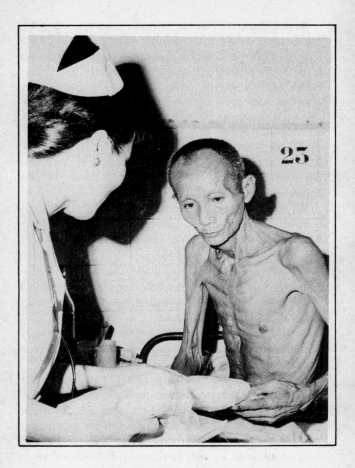

Food for the hungry—
a general's widow serves a refugee.

And British missionary Morris, whose book grew out of one single transforming experience—when a Zambian dropped dead of hunger just outside his front door—adds these words: "Obscenity is a strong word, but I know no other so apt. Obscenity is the jewelled ring on a bishop's finger. It is the flash of my gold wristwatch from under the sleeve of my cassock as I throw dirt on the coffin of a man who died from starvation, murmuring, the while, the most asinine words in the English language—'Since it has pleased almighty God to take to himself our brother.'"

We'll take a long look at that book by Colin Morris a little later. For the moment let's just examine the kind of obscenity he is talking about.

We have already noted this one tremendous basic: that whereas it has taken all the years of time past to bring us to our present world population total—all the centuries which have rolled by—in a few short years this world will double.

Somewhere around 2004, this already hungry planet of ours will have twice as many people on it as it has right now.

Dr. Albert Sabin, developer of the polio vaccine which bears his name, made this statement as quoted in the *Toronto Star-News:* "If changes are not made now, by the year 2,000 there is doubt as to whether we will survive. By that time there will be 700,000 million peoples in the world and 500,000 of them will be starving, uneducated and totally desperate."

What Dr. Sabin is remembering is that most of the population increase in this burgeoning world of ours is going to come in the underdeveloped (or as we are supposed to put it somewhat more euphemistically, the "developing") areas of our world, where hunger is already a present-tense reality. As Colin Morris puts it, again in *Include Me Out:* "In the next twenty-five years, the population of the world will double, and for every bonny, healthy child born on our side of the barricade, ninety-nine skinny ones will pop up on the other side."

True, there are indications that the United States is approaching a birthrate which would *eventually* sustain ZPG (zero population growth). The 1972 birth totals were the lowest since 1945. But the U.S. Census Bureau reminds that this rate would have to be sustained *well into the next century* before ZPG would be sustained.

And this again is not the problem. The tragic fact is that the parts of the world which can least afford it—the already underfed and malnourished developing nations—are the ones which continue to show meteoric rise in population.

It is against this background that the brothers Paddock insist: "There is neither a new agricultural method nor is there a birth-control technique on the horizon which can avert the inevitable famines."[6]

Rear Admiral Lewis L. Strauss, former adviser to five American presidents and previously the chairman of the Atomic Energy Commission, has stated that his greatest concern for the future is that worldwide population growth will be so steep that the number of mouths to feed will outstrip food production.

"Then you have starvation," Admiral Strauss told the Associated Press service. "This is what is staring us in the face."

Quotes like these can be multiplied, of course, and they will be found in abundance as we hurtle through history to that showdown moment when the world goes to its cupboard and finds it bare.

But what about the present? Admittedly, the quotations above have to do with a period of destiny still ahead of us in point of time. That crisis period grows closer every moment, but perhaps you still find some measure of comfort in the fact that it is still future?

Friend, I have news for you. Startling news. Bad news. The *times of the famines* are here. Now.

I doubt that this will surprise you too much. Take a look at your daily paper. (I stopped to do that just now, as I write these words, and one of the first items I saw reported "one of the worst droughts since biblical times," and affecting more than 30 million people in French-speaking West Africa. The item reports that a million people are short of food and "starvation deaths are being reported.")

For years I have read and clipped the reports of the increasing pockets of need around the world, and in recent months my concern has deepened as I have seen how those reports have multiplied.

Here are just a few headlines from newspaper reports I have clipped around the world, all recent as these words are written:

"Afghanistan Uses Camels to Save People from Starvation."⁷

"Crisis Threat in Indonesia Rice Shortage" (AP dispatch from Djakarta).

"Food Output to Fall in Developing Nations"

(from Rome, quoting a release from the UN's Food and Agricultural Organization, FAO).

"Starving Brazilians Loot Shops for Food" (a Reuters report from Brasilia, which I happened to clip half-a-world away in Bangkok, Thailand).

But all those are just words. Translate them into people—flesh and blood people like that woman I saw in the streets of Managua. It was only a few days after the dreadful earthquake had leveled that once great city. The food lines had been set up; supplies were being distributed. But there were just too many people, too many outstretched eager hands.

This woman had come expectantly, holding in her hands a big tin basin she had salvaged from the wreckage of her home. She had stood for a long time in the hot sun, but now the trucks had come and gone and—like perhaps two-thirds of those in line—she was left to stand there with her still-empty basin.

She didn't know who I was, but she saw me watching her, and perhaps my face reflected the deep hurt I felt as I shared her despair. "Please, sir," she cried out in a rapid torrent of Spanish, "tell me—what shall I say to my children? They wait for me at home. They are so hungry. They pray that their mother will come home with food for their empty stomachs. PLEASE—WHAT SHALL I TELL THEM?"

A moment later another man confronted me. He was one of the fortunate ones who had received some food, but he held it in his hand and waved it for me to see: a can of beans, a can of corn, a tiny portion of rice. And he held out something else: a snapshot of his thirteen children. "Señor, I am grateful for this food, but what can I do? There is not enough

27

for all. How can I decide who can eat and who cannot?"

And five minutes later, on that same hot morning in Managua, my associates and I bent anxiously over the prostrate form of a young mother. I tried to question her distraught husband, but he just pointed at his mouth and shook his head negatively. Someone else translated it for me: "His wife has fainted. She is just hungry, so hungry."

I see in my mind the people I have described above, and I also see that little boy in Haiti. He rubs his distended stomach, and he says it over and over, "Please, Papa. I am so hungry."

I see that woman on an unnamed battlefield in Laos. Over the next hill is the famed "Plain of the Jars," and in the distance the big guns boom. Laos, next door neighbor to Vietnam, has its own "forgotten war"; I am there because I have heard that there are people in the area who have been trapped for long months in the fighting and who have no food. We have just landed in a helicopter, and are wondering what to do. Now over the little hill stumbles the reeling figure of a Laotian woman. She is moaning and crying as she staggers along and then falls to her knees before us.

I cannot understand her, so I turn to the interpreter beside me. "She is—demented. She is not right in the head," he says.

"But what is she saying?"

"Oh, she is saying that she is hungry. She has no food, she has been a long time without food."

Somewhere on a tape cassette I have the moaning cry of that woman. But I don't need the tape to

28

remember it. It is recorded forever on the ears of my heart.

That's what it is all about.

People—*people*—like these.

And like that little boy in Cambodia. He has been brought to the refugee camp from an area where there has been heavy fighting. For many weeks his area has had no real food. His little arms and legs are pathetically thin. You may not believe this. I do not blame you if you don't. Your world and mine are very different. But I take thumb and forefinger and gently circle that pencil-thin ankle. I move my hand up that skin-and-bones little leg and—still circling it just with thumb and forefinger—I can move my hand freely over his little knee and far up his thigh.

"Doctor," I say to the Cambodian official with me (and I know my voice shakes as I ask the question), "how old is this boy?"

"He is nine. Nine years old."

So I circle a little boy's leg which is really a little baby's leg in my trembling hand—and I ask God to please, please, *please* somehow let me help.

That's what it is all about.

I can't remember who said or wrote the words. But I agree with them: *"Hunger—anywhere—is a disgrace to humanity."*

Hunger. It's a six-letter word. An ugly, six-letter obscenity.

4

Hunger in the
Midst of Plenty

*"All wild animals and birds and fish
will be afraid of you," God told him;
"for I have placed them in your power, and
they are yours to use for food, in addition
to grain and vegetables." (Genesis 9:2,3)*

"The hunger problem in the world is best described as a *nutrition* problem, and is therefore basically a medical concern."

Those words from my good friend Dr. J. Raymond Knighton, president of Medical Assistance Programs, sum up a major aspect we cannot overlook.

We get concerned, and rightly, about the fact that more than 12,000 people starve to death each day. But we also need to recognize that over three out of five people throughout the world do not receive balanced nutrition.

A powerful 24-page booklet you should read is titled *The Protein Gap*. It is issued by the Bureau of Technical Assistance of AID (the Agency for International Development of the U.S. Government).

Incidentally, let me right here pause for a long bow in the direction of AID. I have seen its work throughout the world, have met with its people on innumerable occasions in many different countries—

32

People in need are closer than you think.

and overall have found them highly motivated, very capable and usually down-to-earth. In this curious day when the "in" thing is to debunk relief and rehabilitation efforts and foreign aid in general, I want to salute AID (and its Canadian counterpart, CIDA) for its tremendous contributions worldwide.

Now, back to *The Protein Gap*. It summarizes the world nutritional crisis in two paragraphs on page 2:

"In the developing countries, some 20 percent of the population is *undernourished*. This means that one person in five does not receive enough food of any kind, that his intake of calories is much less than it ought to be.

"But a far larger proportion, no less than 60 percent, is *malnourished*—and this is much more the alarming figure."[8]

The booklet goes on to point out that: "The 60 percent figure for the underdeveloped populations masks an even grimmer reality. It is found in the fact that the needs of pre-school children and of nursing and pregnant women for balanced nutrition—above all for protein—are much higher than for the rest of the population."

Let's stop for a moment to consider the particularly critical aspect of the effects of long-term malnourishment on the brain development of a child in the first three or four formative years of his life. Without wanting to sound a cheaply alarmist note, or above all to sound callous in the connotation of a sweeping statement, I should remind you of this incredible possibility: that the years of the famines ahead may see not only multiplied millions starving to death, but a literal "planet of the apes" being established

34

in those areas where millions of children are being born into a world which can only offer them drastically inadequate nutrition.

We are told that the brain accomplishes 80 percent of its growth in the first three years of a child's life. Dr. Paul R. Ehrlich and Ann H. Ehrlich sum it up: "This rapid brain growth is primarily a result of protein synthesis (more than 50 percent of the dry weight of brain tissue is protein). When protein is not available in the diet to supply the amino acids from which brain proteins are synthesized, the brain stops growing. Apparently it can never regain the lost time. Not only is head size reduced in a malnourished youngster, but the brain does not fill the cranium."[9]

The Ehrlichs point out that: "Studies in Central and South America have established a strong correlation between nutritional levels and physical and mental development in pre-school and school-age children. Among underprivileged youngsters studied in rural Mexico, height and mental achievement were positively correlated; all these children were near the lower end of the height and mental achievement scale for their ages, indicating that their development was affected by their nutrition" (pp. 76,77).

The Protein Gap underscores the problem: "It is estimated that 80 percent of the pre-school children in rural India suffer from malnutritional dwarfism. There is evidence that chronic malnourishment may result in slowed learning ability and low productivity in later life."

Quotations such as these could be multiplied, of course, and our discussion at this point could quickly become more boringly academic and tedious. Let me therefore just remind you of two basics:

(1) We are talking about real flesh-and-blood children, who have as much right to normal physical and mental development as your children and mine.

(2) All this may come much closer to home than you realize. There are all kinds of studies to show widespread malnutrition and clinical deficiency diseases in our western world—in our developed countries as well as in the developing. Much of this, of course, can be traced to ignorance and neglect as well as poverty. A child in a wealthy home can be malnourished, if his meals are not intelligently planned and supervised.

A recent report from the U.S. Department of Agriculture asserted that *40 million people* in the United States have diets that provide inadequate nutrition. As might be expected, the report pointed out the critical nature of this problem among the poor—but it also maintained that at least 37 percent of households in the U.S. with incomes over $10,000 had diets below recommended daily allowances for one or more nutrients.

We obviously cannot begin to give this subject adequate treatment in a sketchy chapter of this nature. There is no end to the books on nutrition; newspapers these days often provide much helpful information; your family doctor will be glad to counsel you.

Just remember that the big hunger problem in the world is the nutritional crisis . . . that millions of children are the tragic victims . . . and that your family and mine can have nutritional problems.

5

Promises, Promises

*They are like clouds blowing over dry
land without giving rain, promising much,
but producing nothing. (Jude 12)*

Kevin's eyes opened wide as he took a big bite of hamburger. "Hey, this is great!" came my son's somewhat muffled words. "Just like we get at the drive-in!"

His mother and I looked at each other in amusement. We had been waiting a little apprehensively for his reaction, for the steadily rising food prices had driven us to an experiment. And now we knew a little something about that drive-in, for the "hamburger" was really a mixture—part ground beef but also part soy.

We explained this to Kevin, of course, but the explanation didn't seem to faze him a bit. We had matched the drive-in's vaunted quality! We had also saved a bit of money, and had given him a meal which lacked little if anything in protein content.

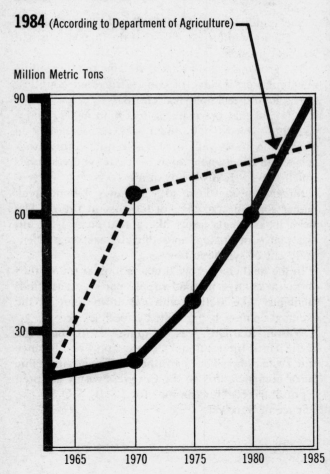

WHEN THE U.S. CANNOT FEED THE WORLD

- - - Grain that the U.S. could produce over and above the amounts needed for domestic use and commercial exports.

▬▬▬ Additional food needed in 66 developing countries

1984 (According to Department of Agriculture)

Million Metric Tons

When Lorraine and I were alone a little later, I shook my head and chuckled. "We really had him fooled for a moment!"

"Yes, and by the way—how did you like the bacon bits on the tossed salad?"

I looked at her with growing suspicion. "You mean—?"

She nodded affirmatively. "Right. That was soy, too. The only difference was that the 'bacon' bits had no meat in them at all!"

The growing world hunger problem and deepening nutritional crisis have of course triggered countless scientific and technological efforts.

It is said that there are no less than 48,000 major scientific projects now under way to increase food production, to "farm" the seas, to render edible products which are not now eaten, to create synthetic foods which are not really foods at all.

Imagine sitting down to a big juicy T-bone steak dinner some day in the not too distant future. The steak looks great, tastes like a real steak . . . but it is really an analog, an artificial steak created entirely out of synthetic fibers.

In the next chapter we'll take a look at the world's efforts to enlarge its food supply per se. At the moment just take a stroll with me down some of the exciting avenues being built by food science.

Washington, D.C. was in August, 1970, the scene of the Third International Congress on Food Science and Technology. That's a rather stuffy and academic bit of nomenclature, so the Congress wisely adopted a popularized "nickname" for itself: S.O.S.—the Science of Survival.

Look at just a few of the titles of the papers presented there under the heading of "New Sources of Proteins":

"Soybean flours and grits."

"Potential of Cottonseed: Products, Composition and Use."

"Rapeseed and Sunflower Protein."

"Preparation, Characterization and Evaluation of Coconut Protein."

"Limitations and Scope of Oilseed Proteins."

"Fish Protein Concentrate."

"Single Cell Protein."

"Algal and Other Microbial Isolated Proteins."

Now those may not mean very much to you technically, but at least they may add to a bit of encouragement. A host of dedicated people and organizations are working on our hunger/nutrition problem. Some are basically idealistic; some primarily concerned with research as a goal; others have admitted and legitimate commercial aims. But at least they're working on it!

In many parts of the world in the developing nations, food preservation and storage is a very critical issue. Transportation is inadequate; refrigeration limited or perhaps nonexistent. A friend of mine in India, for example, insists that this is a large part of their problem. Even when some large areas of India have food sufficient for their own needs with a surplus which could be shared with others, it is impossible to utilize this in other areas because of the transportation and preservation problems. So India is developing freeze-dry and heat-dry processes which

41

will enable certain foods to be kept for long periods of time without refrigeration.

Have you tried the freeze-dry foods? I've had peas which looked like unappetizing, colorless little marbles, but which, when water was added, regained their size and color and taste. I've had meat patties which looked like flat pieces of cardboard, but which miraculously regained their normal appearance and taste when the water which had been removed by freeze-dry processing was replaced.

"The only problem is that these are still basically gourmet foods," says a food-science-engineer friend of mine. "This is the sort of thing you buy out of curiosity or to take hunting or fishing. But it is still a deluxe process which is far away from being a real solution to the hunger problem in the developing nations or the price problem in the developed."

And therein lies the problem. The search goes on, intensified as we shall see in the next chapter by agricultural research and the drive for the "green revolution."

In the blunt realism of their *Famine—1975!* (one of the most significant and prophetically accurate books of recent times), the brothers Paddock take a long look at the various scientific and technological "panaceas" proposed as solutions to the world hunger/nutrition crisis.

Paul Paddock spent twenty-one years in the U.S. Foreign Service. His brother William is an experienced agronomist, who also has lived and worked in the underdeveloped nations for many years.

Together they examine the various hopeful claims put forth by the food technologists, and then conclude: "The time left before the famines and civil unrest is too short a period to carry through those projects which today are in the test tubes. Even with the most ideal conditions of adequate financing, adequate personnel, adequate government support, adequate public understanding, time has run out."[10]

Technology *may* have the answer—thirty or forty or fifty years from now. I personally could be somewhat optimistic about that. But—I remind again that *today's hunger pains aren't satisfied by tomorrow's promises.*

Just ahead of us is the deadly parenthesis when population catches up with food supply and then exceeds it, and the day-by-day and painful reality of the hunger of that period will not be assuaged by the shining hopes and claims of a "tomorrow" still a few decades down the track.

As the Paddocks put it so pointedly:

"All evidence shows there is no possibility that sufficient new technology will be developed through research in time to avert new widespread famine.

"Some day the research will happen.

"In medical circles they do not say, '*if* we get a cure for cancer,' they say, '*when* we get a cure.' But this is no help to the man now suffering from cancer."

6

A Tale of
Two Countries

*"The ground is parched and cracked for lack
of rain; the farmers are afraid." (Jeremiah 14:4)*

"Across the face of India last week," reported
Newsweek, "angry mobs were on the march. In Agra,
they looted grain cars. In Bombay, they smashed the
cars of the rich. In Limdi, they plundered a government warehouse. And in the town of Tumsar, they
stormed the home of a local politician, seized tons
of rice and cattle feed that he had been hoarding
and stoned to death a policeman who tried to stop
them—dragging his body through the streets in a
ghoulish parade of hunger."

Such are the results of real starvation-level hunger,
and the account above again brings to mind the words
of Isaiah 8:21, "And because they are hungry they
will rave and shake their fists at heaven and curse
their King and their God."

What produced the famine in India and the back-
lash of violence? Under the heading, "The Year of

So little to feed so many.

the Famine," the *Newsweek* account went on to say: "Their land parched by drought, their crops dead and their cattle dying, some 200 million Indians face the threat of a disastrous famine in the months ahead . . . what one expert has called 'the worst famine in living memory.' "

This is India, ironically hailed just a few short years ago as the prime example of the "green revolution." India—the scene for so many years of so many pilot projects and such intensified research in agricultural and food development production.

We have already cited India with its seemingly inexorable population march as a prime example of how people—too many people—can drain the resources of a great land.

But we must not leave the impression that only a huge population mass such as this can experience famine. Half a world away from India is little Haiti, which has often been described as perhaps "the poorest place on earth."

"Haiti is hunger," summarizes one book *(Haiti—The Politics of Squalor).* And it quotes *Holiday* magazine in a 1965 description which still applies: "At any hour of day or night, wherever you go, people are stripping sugar cane, peeling bananas, crunching bits of fried pork, buying food, selling it at every corner, eating and being still hungry. Even the skinny, spitting lizards work their mouths constantly."

Comparisons are invidious; oversimplifications are unfair and dangerous. But if we pause to take a look at these two countries—on different sides of the world, diametric opposites in overall population—they may at least help to bring into focus another aspect of our study: the frantic, worldwide agricultural development scramble, and its failure to date.

Consider these basics about India:

Its burgeoning population, second largest in the world, is moving steadily toward the billion mark, slated to arrive there sometime in 1992-93.

It is significant among the nations of the earth as "the bellwether that shows the path which the others are following. The hungry nation that today refuses to heed India's history will be condemned to relive it. The future of mankind is being ground out in India."[12]

Its illiteracy is rated as high as 68 percent, a factor which must be reckoned with as very much a part of the agri-development problem. Progressiveness and literacy go hand in hand.

Its pest problem. It has been estimated that as much as 50 percent of the food India grows is lost to rodents, insects, vermin and birds. (This figure can be challenged, and it is impossible to fix an exact percentage. But the pest problem in India is gargantuan, and is no doubt linked in significant measure to a religious-cultural attitude among many of its millions which venerates life and hesitates to kill even the pest-enemies.)

Its poverty. This may seem at first glance to be an example of putting the proverbial cart before the equally proverbial horse. Which came first—the famine or the poverty? The poverty or the famine? But the economic aspect of the world hunger problem cannot be overlooked, and India, the bellwether, illustrates this facet along with the others listed above. Following an earlier (and smaller scale) famine in

1964-66, India experienced good rains and bumper crops. But next she experienced what one writer termed "India's crisis of plenty." The homegrown food was there, but people had no money to buy it. "The key word is poverty," commented Gordon Bridger and Maurice de Soissons in their somewhat hopeful *Famine in Retreat.* "The root of this Indian situation is a basic economic factor of great magnitude and signal importance, which is often overlooked or ignored. It is that poor people do not earn enough to buy their food requirements."[13]

Population density, illiteracy, pests, the poverty-hunger cycle—these combine to form the *chronic* problem of a country like India. And then actual famines are precipitated when these standing problems are compounded by severe droughts, other natural calamities or socio-political factors (such as India's heroic care of ten million refugees from the then East Pakistan in 1971).

And this analysis brings us to little Haiti: an India in microcosm.

Population? Tiny Haiti with its 10,700 square miles (about the size of the State of Maryland) has a population density rivaling (perhaps exceeding) that of India or China, the two largest nations.

Illiteracy? Haiti has one of the world's lowest levels of functional literacy—between 7 and 10 percent. Turn that around—and it means that ninety to ninety-three out of every one hundred people cannot read.

Poverty? Per capita income is often a misleading figure, especially in a tiny country such as Haiti where a wealthy few can make percentages virtually meaningless. But at best the average Haitian has an annual per capita income of from $67 to $80. Life expectancy averages around 33 years.

Yes, there are many similarities between massive India and mini Haiti. In addition to those cited above, there are transportation difficulties. Food may be available in one area, but in short supply in another. In India, the transportation problem grows out of its sheer size; in Haiti out of an incredibly poor road system which can isolate communities located only a few miles from each other.

And both vast India and tiny Haiti have complex water and irrigation problems.

As these words are written, India's crisis situation is basically drought-induced, compounded by its wall-to-wall people.

And Haiti? "The peaks and sides of all but her highest mountains have been denuded of trees for fuel, and, with the help of violent tropic storms, the richer topsoils. Her rivers consequently run brown, clogged with the humus and detritus of severe ecological neglect. There is little terracing and even less contour plowing. . . ." A veteran missionary summarizes: "Water development is high on the list of priorities for Haiti since it is the key to animal husbandry and the general good health of the people."

All of this adds up, of course, to an admittedly sketchy comparison. Books and books can be written (and have in fact been written) about both these countries; there are multitudinous studies which could be quoted.

We must pause to give credit where credit is due: to the sincere governmental efforts of both these countries (Haiti's of more recent vintage, following the recent major political changes); to the U.S.-based foundations which have extended major help (particularly in the case of India); and to the many splendid voluntary agencies and missionary societies which have with faithfulness "plugged away" in the face of seemingly insurmountable physical/geographical obstacles.

We must also acknowledge that the best efforts of governments and foundations and agencies and individuals can wither away to nothing in the face of drought or other major natural calamity.

So what then are we saying? One conclusion is at least we should guard against false optimism and extravagant claims.

It was not too long ago that India was being acclaimed as the great illustration of hope in the realm of agricultural development. The vaunted "green revolution" there was cited as what technology could accomplish worldwide in the use of miracle strains of rice and wheat, algae farming, hydroponic farming, new-type fertilizers, desalinization—and similar proposed panaceas.

But today's headlines tell the tragic story.

And India and Haiti both underscore another negative lesson. We tend to forget that India once was so prosperous, well-watered and fertile that Diodorus of Sicily could describe it in the first century B.C. as a land where "famine has never visited," and write of "there never being any lack of food among them."

Georg Borgstrom in *The Hungry Planet* tells us that in 1769, *five out of six people in India were well-fed!* In 1969, two hundred years later, only one out of fifty-four could be considered well-fed, and seven out of the fifty-four were starving, and forty-six malnourished.

And Haiti? "On the eve of the French Revolution Haiti, then called Saint-Dominique, was the veritable Pearl of the Antilles. It was France's most prosperous colony, it outranked any of the British possessions in their contributions to the wealth of the mother country, and in contemporary as well as historic lights, Haiti was the wealthiest European outpost in the New World."[14]

Isn't there a lesson here for us—for the developed nations of the world?

As I review all this, and think of the present needs, I see again the compassionate face of missionary Ed Shreve, a lanky Virginian, and a veteran of service in Haiti, and hear his earnest words:

"Somehow we must get whole milk for the babies. I remember a girl from our area—only 16—who got in trouble in Gonnaive. She had no money, but some people there took pity on her, and put her on a sailboat going near her village. They just laid her on the beach—and then her parents came and put her on a burro to take her home."

And I guess Ed Shreve, man's man that he is, wouldn't mind my telling you that his eyes were full of tears and his voice broke a bit as he added:

"She and the baby both died. It was awful—seeing that little baby's mouth just move open and shut like it was begging for milk. . . ."

I remember too his description of an earlier famine: "I was driving down the road and saw this old woman just staggering along, weak from hunger. I had no food. All I had was ten cents, and of course I gave that to her. Then I saw another woman just as bad off—and so I called to that first woman who was still in sight and told her she must share the ten cents with the other. . . ."

The Lord said, "Thank you, Ed, for the ten cents you gave Me. It was all you had, but you gave it to Me."

Ed, wondering, replied, "Lord, when did I ever give You ten cents?"

And Jesus answered softly, "Inasmuch as you gave ten cents unto one of the least of these, you gave it to Me."

7

"And There Will Be ... Earthquakes in Many Places"

*Thou hast made the land quake
and torn it open; it gives
way and crumbles into pieces.
(Psalm 60:2, NEB)*

"I walk through the rubble, block after block, shaking my head in disbelief. I have walked through war and disaster many times before, but never have I seen utter devastation to compare with this."

The above paragraph opens a magazine article in *Christian Life* (March 1973), reporting on the devastating earthquake which shattered Managua, Nicaragua, in the early morning of December 23, 1972.

Just back from Bangladesh when word came of this new disaster, I left for Nicaragua as soon as possible. As I re-read the words above, which I wrote while still in Nicaragua, the heartbreak and horror of that situation crowd in upon me once again.

To fully understand this hungry planet which we are studying, we must take a long look at the complex matter of earthquakes (and their first cousins, the volcanoes). But let's be sure it is a *compassionate* look.

This was once a home.

Let's remind ourselves again that the full significance of volcanoes and earthquakes is seen only when we relate these to people.

We might parallel or paraphrase that old chestnut of a question: "If a tree falls in a forest and there's no one around to hear it, can we really say that it makes a sound?" (Sound in this trick-question case is of course understood to be only that which happens in an ear which is reacting to the shock waves triggered. Which came first: the sound or the ear?)

Our question, a sincere one, is: "If an earthquake or volcano occurs in an absolutely uninhabited place, one which has no economic or agricultural or other elements which would affect people, what difference does it make?"

Well, when an earthquake hits a populous area, a Peru or Los Angeles or Managua, it *does* make a difference, and that difference is all wrapped up in people.

Read along with me a bit in that *Christian Life* article:

"You know the statistics of Managua: The thousands who died (some estimates say as many as 12,000; we may never know for sure) . . . the multitudes who fled the city in the pre-Christmas dawn as all their world tumbled down around them . . . the 500,000-plus who according to the U.S. Public Health Service will need supplementary feeding from now until October.

"I walk along, and a fragment of a song tugs at my memory, its calypso beat oddly out of place in this silent city of death: 'Managua, Nicaragua, is a beautiful town. . . .'

58

"A beautiful town? No, not now. Its buildings have crumpled into ruins; its streets lie in eerie silence; its air is heavy with the acrid smell of smoke and the unmistakable stench of death.

"Over there is a home. It's a neat, modern little dwelling which could fit into your neighborhood or mine—in Montrose, Pennsylvania or Montrose, California. The brown door is intact, unscratched—but now it opens to nothingness, except to broken walls and broken hopes.

"And here in the street is a tiny sandal. Did you lose it, little one, as you fled in terror? Or perhaps it fell to the ground as a grieving parent carried your lifeless little body through the streets.

"So I walk on, and my heart aches as I see the wall-to-wall desolation, and realize what it represents in tears and terror, in heartache and loss, in disease and hunger."

Earthquakes, one might say, we have always with us; and the prophetic Scriptures promise that they'll continue to occur "in many places" until the end of time.

Earthquakes aren't new. Ancient history tells us that Constantinople (now Istanbul) was devastated by an earthquake in A.D. 557, and then completely razed by another in A.D. 936.

That's going back quite a long ways into the past, but we can look back even further. Every schoolboy knows (well, we all *used* to know about it, and I suspect that the batting average today would still be pretty good) about Pompeii. The archives tell us that Pompeii was destroyed by that mighty eruption of Mt. Vesuvius in A.D. 79, and this is of course the familiar reference. But the record also shows that Pompeii had been very severely damaged by an earthquake earlier, in A.D. 63.

Some of the quakes past have taken an incredible toll in human life. An earthquake in Japan in 1703 killed over 200,000 people. Terrible though that is to contemplate, a quake a few years later (1737) had claimed over 300,000 lives. But towering over these as a monument of heartbreak is the 1556 quake in Shensi, China, which reportedly saw 830,000 die.

Many, many major such happenings could be detailed, but I suspect that most of us don't need much convincing to accept the fact that they are a literal, frightening reality today—and a source of deep concern about tomorrow.

Some of us can remember the 1946 quake in the Aleutian Islands which saw 173 people killed and property damage in Hawaii exceeding $25 million. Many others will recall the massive quake in Alaska in 1964, where 115 died and property damage was estimated at an astronomical $311 million.

And fresh in the minds of many of us is the 1971 earthquake in the Los Angeles, California area. (I suppose I could mention in passing that the house in which these words are being written still displays some "souvenir" cracks of that event.)

With all this in mind, it stands to reason that scientists are working overtime to study the earthquake phenomenon, and to develop via supersensitive recorders and laser beams some method of *predicting* when and where major quakes will occur.

For a colorful, vivid, enlightening and yet completely sobering view of this entire consideration, see the *National Geographic* for January 1973. (The timing of this particular study must set some kind of record for editorial intuition, for the issue had just been printed and mailed when the Managua quake occurred and claimed the interest of the world.)

Familiar as the earthquake is to all of us, we may never have stopped to consider a most fundamental question. Just what *is* an earthquake?

"The earth never rests. It is constantly shaken by all manner of natural and man-made disturbances—surf beating on the beach, the ocean of air exerting changing pressures on the surface, rain striking the ground, wind shaking trees, buildings and mountains. Even trains rattling along their tracks and traffic rumbling along the highway cause part of the earth's surface to move a few thousandths, or a few ten-thousandths, of an inch. These vibrations are called microseisms ('little shakings'), and they are occurring in one form or another at all times and all places.

"*Earthquakes* are caused by the rupturings of rocks at, or below, the earth's surface. These ruptures result in sudden, short-lived motions of the ground which originate in a small region and then spread out from it in all directions. Earthquakes are distinguished from microseisms by the fact that the latter are continuous vibrations, while earthquakes begin suddenly and have more or less definite endings."[15]

The *National Geographic* treatise mentioned above expands on the above textbook-type definition to present an exciting theory. The shifting crust of the earth, it maintains, actually consists of some twenty huge segments called "plates." These moving plates, which vary from thirty to one hundred miles in thickness, are like gargantuan rafts which carry the continents and the ocean basins on their backs. They slide around on a hot, semiplastic layer and earthquakes and volcanic eruptions occur, says the article, when "the rigid plates grind and crush together."

All this may or may not make interesting reading, depending on the degree of scientific interest you have. Once again, we come back to the fundamental fact that all of this process would make very little difference if the world were uninhabited.

The problem is that on top of those continents on top of those plates are buildings—and in those buildings are *people.* Some of those buildings are homes, some are stores and factories, others are hospitals and churches. All of them relate to people.

Considered from this point of view, the earthquake problem takes on specific dimensions. It becomes important, for example, to develop methods of *predicting* earthquakes.

Japan, Russia and the United States are pooling research in developing earthquake forecasts. An Associated Press dispatch (datelined Menlo Park, Calif., Jan. 7, 1973) says that by 1983 "earthquake warnings as reliable and precise as hurricane warnings will be feasible."

Some of the efforts being made to develop an early warning system for predicting earthquakes read like science fiction. For example, in Boulder, Colorado, in an abandoned gold mine, a laser beam is fired through a 100-foot tube to detect movements or even vibrations in the earth's crust. The instrument can spot such infinitesimal variations as *20 trillionths of an inch* in the earth's crust, which is said to be the same as measuring a change of a hundredth of an inch in the distance from the earth to the sun!

So the seismic forecasters develop their new but most impressive craft. Meanwhile, imperceptibly as far as we are concerned, those big plates on which we ride continue to move and bump and threaten.

Now, let's bring all this down to focus. What does all this mean to us?

1. It's time to (let's use that timeworn phrase) *be prepared.* Every city, particularly those along a major earthquake fault, should have a thorough disaster alert plan which includes such basics as communications, emergency food and medical care, evacuation and temporary housing. It is estimated that the earthquake which shook the Los Angeles area on February 9, 1971 could have killed as many as 80,000 to 100,000 people. Providentially, the quake hit only the edge of the sprawling megalopolis. It came in the early morning, before the usual multiplied thousands jammed the streets and freeways. A huge dam almost gave way—almost, but not quite. Had it collapsed, the earthquake (which claimed only 64 lives) could have been one of the major disasters of all time. What will happen in Los Angeles, in San Francisco, in you-name-it, when the next big shake comes?

2. It is equally important that *you* have your plan. Take a moment for a Family Disaster Checklist. How many of the following do you have?

—Emergency food rations, stored in some safe place away from house or garage (which might collapse in a quake).

—Small portable radio, with fresh (and extra) batteries.

—Flashlights, also with batteries.

—Tents.

—Blankets.

—First aid kits.

—Simple medicines.

—An agreed-upon place (or places) to meet other members of your family, or other close relatives or friends, if your city experiences some major disaster.

Sound far-fetched? Chances are the average person in Managua would have smiled, too, and brushed such inquiries aside—if you had presented the list to him on December 22, 1972.

But I remember the heartache, the confusion, the medical needs I saw in Managua during those hectic last days of December, and I ache anew as I remember the pathetic sight of people searching for their loved ones in the wreckage.

3. We must face the fact that this world of ours will have its earthquakes, its volcanoes, its cyclones and hurricanes and typhoons and floods. These natural disasters, remember, are the ones which catch us least prepared. Wars usually cast some kind of ugly shadow before them; their great refugee migrations are somewhat predictable. But the sudden Nicaraguan or Peruvian earthquake, an East Pakistan cyclone or volcanic eruption in Bali—these are tragedies which will come like the proverbial thief in the night, and for which *we must be prepared*. Wherever the next major disaster happens, it will affect neighbors of ours, in this shrinking world.

Today, as these words are written, we are assembling specific emergency food rations and canned water, and working with sister agencies to have similar medical supplies, palletized and ready for instant airlift to the next major disaster area. But these are only Bandaids—mere emergency first aid.

I remember discussing with General and Mrs. Somoza, who were personally directing the aid to earthquake victims in Managua, an all-too-familiar pattern in disaster situations. First, there is usually an initial lag. (In the Managua earthquake, fortunately, this was very short. U.S. AID teamed up with the American military to rush very substantial supplies of food and medicine into Nicaragua. The political situation, where uniformed U.S. military were welcome, and the geographic proximity of Nicaragua to the United States helped in no small measure, of course, but all in all it was a very commendable operation.)

Secondly, in the usual pattern, there is the great response of compassion from around the world. Sometimes zeal outpaces good sense, as in Bangladesh where thousands of *electric* blankets were shipped into a country which is tropic to begin with and where in most cases the nearest electric outlet was a few hundred miles away. But it is still heart-warming to see how the world can respond! I stood in Managua, for example, and watched planes sweeping in with relief cargo—from Mexico, Venezuela, Cuba, Sweden, Germany, Great Britain and the United States. All of these I mention arrived within one forty-minute span on a typical day in the first week following the earthquake.

But, thirdly, the real "crunch" usually comes after a few weeks or even months have elapsed. Five months after the Managua quake, for example, a Christian committee known as CEPAD (in English, the "Evangelical Committee for Development") was providing over 90,000 meals a week for children, the elderly, expectant and lactating mothers. They were planning on at least a full year of continuous program of this magnitude. Meanwhile the rest of the world was beginning to forget. The first great emotional response had died down, and the flood of relief into Nicaragua had slowed to first a stream and then a trickle. But there were still those who remembered, who cared and helped, and so CEPAD could carry on.

As I record that happy fact, I think back to my first departure from Managua after the earthquake. We had rushed there as quickly as possible, had surveyed the needs and found ways to help. Now we were headed home to enlist support, and I found myself wondering. That wondering turned to a prayer as I asked, "Father, will *anybody* really care? There have been so many disasters, so many requests for help. . . ."

A few days later I found my answer. I had spoken in an elementary school in Southern California to a wonderful audience of third, fourth, fifth and sixth graders. I'll never forget their response to the pictures I showed, or the concern and even compassion reflected in their faces and in the questions they asked.

After the assembly period they proudly showed me the large supply of canned goods they had assembled, and formed a happy "bucket brigade" to pass along the boxes and sacks and fill up my station wagon.

And the part I'll always remember, the one which

answered that "Will anybody care?" query of mine, came just a little later when my teen-age son and I were repacking the food for shipment to Nicaragua. As we were separating the beans and the powdered milk and the canned meats and so on, I reached into one box to pull out a little brown paper sack. In it I found an apple, a peanut butter sandwich and a cookie. On the outside of the sack, in a little girl's carefully large printing, the crayoned name "Christi" and "Room 104." Little Christi hadn't brought any canned goods, but her heart had been touched and she wanted to give. *So she had given her own lunch.*

Then I realized what had happened, and I had my answer. Yes, people will always care . . . as long as "a little child shall lead them!"

As I held that little sack in my hands, I confess I looked at it through suddenly misty eyes. For a moment I didn't see just an apple and a dried-up peanut butter sandwich and a cookie. I saw *loaves and fishes,* and heard a divine Voice say it: "Thank you, Christi. I was hungry and you fed Me. When you did it to these My brothers, you were doing it to Me."

Let's face it. The earthquakes and the volcanoes and the other natural disasters will keep on coming, forcing their sudden shock upon our world. Over 900,000 people have been killed by earthquakes alone in the past century, with over $10 billion damage—and we are never more than a year away from a major disaster of this nature.

What's your C.Q. (Compassion Quotient)? Will *you* have a lunch to give?

The Bible Says

*"If you have two coats . . . give one to
the poor. If you have extra food, give
it away to those who are hungry." (Luke 3:11)*

"It has been said that you have looked into more
hungry faces than any other man of our day," said
the reporter, and he added, "I suppose that's why
you are doing what you are—because you have seen
all those hungry people all around the world."

"That's part of it, of course," I replied. "But only
part. Yes, I live with the nightmare of this world's
hunger. I've seen it so many times in so many places.
But the main reason I am doing what I am is because
of this Book." And I held up my Bible.

Let me be very direct, very personal, in this chapter. Over thirty years ago, when I was just a boy, I put
my trust in Jesus Christ as my Lord and Saviour.

Through these past three decades plus, my desire
to serve Him has only intensified. And the more I
come to know Him, the more I want to pattern my
life after His perfect example.

Help for the children.

I watch Jesus as He walks through the pages of Scripture. I watch Him as He not only teaches but reaches—reaches out in love to heal the sick, the lame, the blind. I stand by in amazement as He lovingly deals with the sinner . . . and graciously feeds the hungry.

And day by day I pick up a vibrant volume which never fails to amaze me: the Bible. I look at it now, beside me on the desk as I talk to you in these pages, and I want you to know that I feel a bit like that new convert, a man who had just entered into personal faith in the God of the Bible. This man, so the story goes, declared with fervor, "I believe the Bible from cover to cover!" He thought for a moment, and then added, "And I believe the cover, too, because it says 'Holy Bible' and it is!"

Now, let's face it. Perhaps I lost you with my simple declaration of faith. Perhaps you aren't interested in or acquainted with (that follows!) this Book of books which means so much to me.

Fair enough. I guess you don't have to believe my Bible, or follow any religious teaching for that matter, to be concerned about the needs of others. You certainly don't have to be religious to be concerned about your own future and that of your family in this swelling-and-about-to-burst hungry planet. But if you do make a stand or even a pretense of religious faith, you'd better pause for a moment to see what this implies in terms of personal responsibility.

If you are just afraid of what's ahead, in dwindling food supply and in mounting prices, I suggest you comfort yourself by studying just a bit of what the "Good Book" has to say. It might help. And whoever you are and wherever, I think it should at least be a matter of intellectual curiosity for you to see what this well-worn old Book of mine has to say.

You see, not even all those who read it most and preach it loudest always stop to *hear* all that it says about our responsibilities to our neighbors.

As Dr. Billy Graham is wont to declare, "The Bible says. . . ." Believe it, it does.

It says, for example, that "he who shuts his ears to the cries of the poor will be ignored in his own time of need" (Prov. 21:13). That's something to ponder.

It suggests a basic cause of discontent, on both international and domestic levels: "And because they are hungry they will rave and shake their fists at heaven and curse their King and their God" (Isa. 8:21).

It tells us something about God Himself with words like these, "The kind of fast I want is that you stop oppressing those who work for you and treat them fairly and give them what they earn. I want you to share your food with the hungry and bring right into your own homes those who are helpless, poor and destitute. . . . Feed the hungry! Help those in trouble!" (Isa. 58:6,7,10).

I'm indebted to Continental Air Lines for calling to my attention a verse from the Bible which provided the name for the work in which I am engaged (Food for the Hungry, Inc.). On a little "grace before meals" card distributed by the airline, I found the tremendous self-portrait God paints of Himself in the words of Psalm 146 (verses 6 and 7): "He is the God who

73

keeps every promise, and gives justice to the poor and oppressed, and *food to the hungry."*

I told that newspaper reporter it was looking into the Bible (as well as into all those hungry faces) which provided the focus for my life's work of endeavoring to help the hungry and to help them help themselves.

Yes indeed! As I read my Bible, from Genesis to the Revelation 66 tremendous chapter-books later, it shows me how the love of God reaches out not only to everyone, but to *all* of everyone.

It tells me that the God of the Bible cares not only about the whole world, but the whole man.

And I begin to see what my friend Dr. Bob Pierce meant, when he declared, "We have a right to speak, but we have to *earn* the right to be heard."

Note the very practical and candid observation of Scripture: "But if someone who is supposed to be a Christian has money enough to live well, and sees a brother in need, and won't help him—how can God's love be within *him?* Little children, let us stop just *saying* we love people; let us *really* love them, and *show it* by our *actions"* (1 John 3:17,18).

Let's stop for a moment to clear up one point. Labels have a way of confusing when they should be clarifying, and ordinarily I try to avoid the label which poses semantic complexities and/or theological ramifications and/or regional or national difficulties.

In other words, I'm happy just to be identified as a Christian—as one who has voluntarily committed his life to Christ and who is endeavoring to live and work and love as *He* did and does.

But you go right ahead, if you want to, and label me evangelical or conservative or even fundamentalist. Do that, I mean, as long as you don't take away my right to love this world as my Saviour loves it, and as long as you don't expect me to handle snakes and vipers as part of my worship of the Most Holy God. (I'm not *that* kind of fundamentalist, although I shake my head in loving sympathy and breathe a little prayer just now for misguided people who do think that's what it is all about.)

Why am I saying all this? Because I suspect that someone listening in, as I talk to you, is getting very uncomfortable. He is *not* that person I was talking about back in the beginning of the chapter who is not at all interested in the Bible. No, the one I'm concerned about right now is the one who for a different reason is scratching his head (and the sincere lady doing the feminine equivalent; although come to think of it, I never really have seen any women scratching their heads in this particular sense).

I'm thinking about that person who is so committed to *spiritual* concerns that he gets worried when anyone talks about providing literal food for the physically hungry. This is the kind of person who feels that any kind of relief work or social welfare activity is "social gospel," and insists that we should concentrate our energies on purely spiritual concerns.

Now, I cited my personal evangelical/conservative/fundamentalist stance for just that kind of person. I want you to know I do stand where you do in belief in the Bible—and I do understand how you can fall into this kind of intellectual trap, and do so with the best of intentions.

You see, it was out of that kind of early spiritual background that I began to look into the Bible to

75

try to find God's priorities. When I did so, I saw how clearly and unmistakably it portrays a God whose love reaches out not only to every corner of the world but to every area of man's need.

I found that all the Bible, from beginning to end, pounds out this theme with trip-hammer rapidity and regularity.

So to my brother or sister who tends to be "so spiritually minded that he's no earthly good," I commend the reading of the Scriptures with an open mind and heart.

You may not be able to look with me into hungry faces all around the world, but you can look with me into a Book more than a book which tells us how to react to them and what to do.

Come walk with me through the Scriptures for a moment. I was in Burma recently, and also (in my daily Bible reading) in the book of Proverbs. Let me without comment just list a few of the verses which spoke to me day after day. Remember, I wasn't looking for these verses as a sort of proof text or to list in a book such as this. Reading just for my own heart's good, and to find God's service priorities and responsibilities for myself, I read verses like these:

"To despise the poor is to sin. Blessed are those who pity them" (Prov. 14:21).

"Anyone who oppresses the poor is insulting God who made them. To help the poor is to honor God" (14:31).

"If your enemy is hungry, give him food!" (25:21).

"If you give to the poor, your needs will be supplied" (28:27).

"The good man knows the poor man's rights; the godless don't care" (29:7).

Elsewhere in this book I have quoted other verses I gleaned from Proverbs during just those few days' reading in Burma. There was the charge I took to my own heart, "Speak up for the poor and needy," and those words about a good wife who "sews for the poor, and generously gives to the needy" (both from chapter 31).

Are you still worried about that old bugaboo of the "social gospel"? Heed the warning of Dr. Carl F. H. Henry—contemporary theologian, man of God, good friend. Years ago in his pioneering *The Uneasy Conscience of Modern Fundamentalism,* Dr. Henry reminded us that in revolting against the social gospel, we tend to forget the social imperative. He pointed out that where once the redemptive gospel was a world-changing message, it has been reduced to a world-resisting message by our emphasizing individual salvation and neglecting community responsibility.

Think about this one for a moment, from the pen of my good friend Dr. Sherwood Eliot Wirt: "Dr. Timothy Smith of the University of Minnesota has rendered a service to the church by unearthing a little-known fact about the social gospel: it took its roots not in religious 'liberalism' or skepticism, but in the evangelical revival."[16]

Does this all sound a bit new and heretical? Then consider this testimony from a few years back. In about A.D. 125 the Athenian philosopher Aristides delivered to Emperor Hadrian a defense of the faith which included this description of his fellow Christians:

"They love one another; the widow's needs are not ignored, and they rescue the orphan from the person who does him violence. He who has gives to him who has not, ungrudgingly and without boasting. . . . If they find poverty in their midst and they do not have spare food, they fast two or three days in order that the needy might be supplied with necessities." (Quoted by Dr. Sherwood Eliot Wirt in his *The Social Conscience of the Evangelical.*)

Remember Joe Bayly's remarkable (and tongue-in-cheek) book, *The Gospel Blimp?* As I recall it, and the film based on it, the founders of the blimp ministry had picked out a neighbor who was a sort of symbol of those whom they wanted to reach with the tracts they dropped and the preachments they thundered out from their "pulpit in the sky." But when, in the end of the book, the man comes to faith in Christ, they find that what reached him was friendship and helpfulness. Someone helped him when his wife was sick; someone took him fishing—treated him as a person to be loved, not just as a statistic to be reached.

In the work of the Church around the world, I have seen this love-principle demonstrated many times. Take the example of the Evangelical Church of Vietnam. You could not ask for a more faithful, evangelistic group, preaching the Word for a full half-century. But then came the war, and the Christians, moved by the constraining love of Christ, opened their homes to the homeless and shared their food with the hungry. They walked through the refugee centers and hospitals, I think, really not so much for evangelistic strategy as just in a natural outpouring of Christian love. And the wonderful result was the greatest evangelistic opportunity they have ever known. Thousands in Vietnam have been won to Christ by demonstrated love. In narrating a film on Vietnam, I pointed out that the Christians there move day-by-day through the refugee camps and hospital wards in a ministry of love which says, "Yes—we care about you in eternity. But we also care about you *now.*" Then when it's time for their preaching services, they can go back to those same people to whom they have so convincingly shown the love of Christ and say, "Look—we have shown that we care about you now. Please come and let us tell you about eternity." And they come. In fact, I have heard the Vietnamese Christians and many of the missionaries declare, "These are our greatest days!"

You know, I want to show the love of Christ to people in practical, down-to-earth terms such as we have been talking about.

And I hope you feel the same.

I think it was Dietrich Bonhoeffer who described Jesus Christ as "the man for others." I like that! I hope someday someone will be able to think of me in those terms.

Meet the Press

It occurred to me that it would be well . . .
after thorough investigation
to pass this summary on to you. (Luke 1:3)

At about this point it might be helpful to stop and
pull all this together with a bit of a summary. Let's
do this via the vehicle of a press conference, with
my sharing with you some of the questions commonly
put to me in press, radio and TV interviews, as well
as those I encounter in churches and service clubs,
as well as on the college campus.

In answering those questions, let me by docu-
mented quotations step aside at times to let you hear
from authorities in the various fields.

How serious is the world hunger situation?

It's a crisis today . . . and it will be a tragedy
tomorrow. It may well be that, after our years of
relative plenty, we are about to face the most terrible
"seven lean years" of want our world has ever known.

"We are approaching a global catastrophe through

Waiting their turn.

overpopulation, pollution and poor management of our resources. We must regard the earth as a solitary spaceship with an unknown destination on which 3.5 billion astronauts are traveling through space. These astronauts are abusing the strictly limited raw materials of Spaceship Earth and it is imperative that determined steps be taken at once."—Dr. Wernher von Braun, at the International Astronautical Congress, Vienna, Austria, Oct., 1972.

Does the "population explosion" really pose a threat? Isn't this just theoretical?

Remember, it has taken all the years of time to bring us to our present world-population total. Barring some kind of divine intervention which no one can specifically predict, the world now will double itself within the next thirty years.

"The rising tide of people threatens to deprive the human race of its future. . . . If the world's population continues to expand at the present rate . . . within 120 years the present production of foodstuffs will have to be increased eightfold if the present standards are maintained—and yet these are inadequate for more than half the present number of people."— Georg Borgstrom, *The Hungry Planet.*

But won't "something turn up"? It always has.

Unfortunately, the "somethings" which "turn up" in this present historical context only serve to underscore the alarms. The growing energy crisis, the pressure points of famine around the world, the fuel shortages and rising prices, the drain on the world's resources when volcanoes and earthquakes come—all these are bad, and will only grow worse.

"In reviewing all the proposed panaceas for increasing food production during the next decade, the conclusion is clear: there is no possibility of improving agriculture in the hungry nations soon enough to avert famine. . . . No panacea is at hand to increase the productivity of the land, just as no miracle will arrest the population explosion."—William & Paul Paddock, *Famine—1975!*

"And there will be famines and earthquakes in many places."—The Lord Jesus Christ (Matt. 24:7).

But I don't live in one of the "developing countries"—one of the hungry nations. What does all this mean to me?

Apart from the question of whether or not you are your brother's keeper, and the moral implications involved in that, you must face the fact that your own world will be vastly different in the years just ahead.

Under the heading "Food Prices Linked to Overpopulation," the *Los Angeles Times* (April 6, 1973) quotes a distinguished biologist as saying that we may have already "turned a corner . . . with the boycott of early April (1973) signaling a new way of life at the American dinner table." Interviewing Dr. Garrett Hardin, the paper states that "population is one of his areas of expertise, and he says that the meat shortage, with consequent high prices, is just one more symptom of overpopulation. Demand has outstripped the supply."

Is birth control the answer? What about the moral implications?

"The people who will be hungry tomorrow are

85

already born."—Richard W. Reuter, former Director, Food for Peace Program.

"No decline in world population growth is in prospect. The efforts now being made—encouraging as they are—are in grave danger of being far too little and dangerously late."—Annual Report, Population Reference Bureau, 1967.

"The population explosion—or, to put it more precisely, the collapse of the ecological balance of the human population when medical progress has preceded industrial growth—is one of the most urgent problems facing the human beings of today and is preparing a grievous inheritance for those of tomorrow."—*Development Forum,* UN, May, 1973.

"In the world of today, children are the greatest cause of poverty."—Gunnar Myrdal, Swedish economist.

"Fertility is the blessing and the promise that are based on the union between two beings. In the Bible, children are called the fruits of love, its blessed echo. In connection with children, the biblical texts speak neither of duty or of obligation, but of grace and thankfulness. 'Be fruitful and multiply' is not an order, but a blessing pronounced on love."—André Dumas, professor, Protestant Faculty of Theology, University of Paris, writing on "Population—A Protestant View," *Development Forum,* UN, May, 1973.

"The time is long past due for evangelical Christians to be taking a public stand on the issue of birth control. To add to the spate of volumes is not necessary; what is needed is some indication that there is a Bible-centered point of view in the matter, based on the desire of God for the welfare of man, and on principles of Christian stewardship. At the turn of the century, when evangelicals thought about birth control at all, they condemned it as contrary to nature. Such a position is no longer tenable; the place is simply getting too crowded."—Dr. Sherwood Eliot Wirt, *The Social Conscience of the Evangelical.*

Can't modern technology save the day?

Pessimistic predictions notwithstanding, it is altogether reasonable to assume that technology *may* come up with "the answer" or answers—twenty or thirty years from now. But that will be too late to help the millions suffering and dying in the next nineteen years or so, and the countless other millions facing serious mental retardation because of extreme malnourishment in infancy.

What about the "green revolution"?

"This so-called green revolution is a propagandistic and highly misleading way of describing an annual growth rate of 5 percent in the production of wheat and rice, a growth that is now leveling off and benefiting only certain sections of the farming community in India. . . ."—*The Death of the Green Revolution,* Haslemere Group, April, 1973.

"Three years of cloudless skies have left 20 million peasants in Maharashta destitute. The land is dead; the crop has been almost totally lost; this is perhaps the worst famine in the State's history."—"They Must Not Die," *The Illustrated Weekly of India,* January 7, 1973.

Can't we pin some hope on "farming the seas"?

Dr. Kenneth E. F. Watt of the University of California points to the sea as one natural resource among many which has been over-exploited and endangered. "The technological optimists say that the oceans are an inexhaustible source of food," Dr. Watt admits, but he points to the fact that recent figures showed that fish catches worldwide *decreased* by 5 percent. "Now, the way our effort is increasing and with the increasing technical sophistication of fishing gear, isn't it remarkable that, if the oceans are in fact an inexhaustible source of food, that the catch is actually going down?" Dr. Watt maintains that the food production of the seas is likely to decrease in the future because they are being over-fished and because of the pollution of spawning grounds by such materials as mercury and DDT.—*The National Enquirer.*

"What about those 'unmeasurable riches' in the seas? Unhappily, they have been measured and found wanting. The notion that we can extract vastly greater amounts of food from the sea in the near future is quite simply just another myth promoted by the ignorant or the irresponsible. Wherever I go, people ask me about our 'farming of the sea' and are invariably shocked by my answer. We are not 'farming' the sea today, and to my knowledge there is not a single group in the United States even attempting to go about it. In general, man hunts the sea, and occasionally he herds its animals. About the only planting and harvesting of marine crops that man does is some seaweed culture in Japan, and this is really best viewed as an extension of agricultural techniques into the sea. 'Farming' the open sea will present an entirely different array of problems."—Dr. Paul Ehrlich, *The Population Bomb.*

It's admittedly a cynical question, but don't you think maybe God has his own checks and balances and even the millions who die in the famines and wars and natural disasters are his way of making things even?

If you mean "God" in the literal sense, you have to lay the uncertainties of this question over the specific certainties—the direct commands—of His written Word. If this is true, why does He tell us over and over again that we are to help the poor and feed the hungry?

"Cynical hopes that war will get rid of excess populations are unfounded. The two great wars in this century did little in this respect. Their combined casualties of forty to fifty million are less than the present net annual increase of sixty-five million. All the bombs now in store would not suffice for mass extermination, and to achieve the latter by bombing would be more than our economic resources could stand."—Georg Borgstrom, *The Hungry Planet.*

Incidentally, to expand that last answer a bit, let's call on Borgstrom, professor of Food Science at Michigan State University, to comment on the relationship of world hunger to international unrest and war: "The popular notion that it is the hungry countries that take recourse to war is quite false. A starving people do not have the resources and other prerequisites for war; and history substantiates the other view: it is the countries that are threatened with hunger and a lowering of living standards that resort to war, for example, Japan's invasion of Manchuria, Italy's African conquests, and Germany's plundering of Europe, to cite examples only from our own time. When William Vogt's *Road to Survival* was published in 1948, *Time* in its review stated that if the United States ever would reach the unlikely position of not having enough food for its population because of land shortage, there would be only one remedy: to go out and grab the land it needed!"—*The Hungry Planet*.

Then what do you want us to do?

To begin with, read the next chapter! Carefully. Prayerfully.

10

What Do You Want Us to Do?

The crowd replied, "What do you want
us to do?" "If you have two coats,"
he replied, "give one to the poor. If
you have extra food, give it away to
those who are hungry." (Luke 3:10,11)

I suppose that a very natural question about now
is, "Then what do you want us to do?"

Without further preamble, let me proceed to answer that question very directly:

1. "If you have two coats, give one to the poor.
If you have extra food, give it away to those who
are hungry." I wish I could take credit for that answer
in all its simple profundity, but you perhaps have
already detected that it has a somewhat familiar ring!
Yes, the verse quoted above, at the head of this chapter, is *the* basic answer.

Obviously I can be accused of being simplistic. I
cheerfully accept that label, for this whole complex
matter of world hunger and the global nutritional
crisis ultimately comes down to this as the irreducible
minimum of solution.

The ground is parched and cracked for lack of rain;
the farmers are afraid.   Jeremiah 14:4

Yes, there are those 48,000 major scientific projects, that frantic technological scramble. Technology may well hold the solutions—twenty or thirty years from now. But that adds up to three or four periods of "seven lean years" in the interim—and I repeat that *today's hunger pains are not assuaged by tomorrow's promises.*

For the critical years just ahead, the answers are not found in the hardware of computerized technology, but in the "software" of compassionate concern.

2. Spread the word. Let's face it. A lot of what I have told you in these pages is not all that new. You perhaps could not have quoted all the statistics or marshalled all the quotes, but I suppose you were in general aware of the population crisis, the dwindling food supply and the subsequent collision.

That's just the problem. It is this general awareness which creates the complacency, the lack of concern, the raised eyebrow and backward step when a Larry Ward comes along as another wild-eyed prophet of Malthusian doomsday.

But the simple fact that you have read along this far in the book is a source of encouragement! And if all this begins to make serious sense, why not appoint yourself a committee of one to challenge your community: your family, friends, school, P.T.A., service club, Sunday School class, church or whatever marching-and-chowder society you can influence.

I haven't said this before, but I'll say it now. I hope I'm wrong. Yes, *I hope I am wrong in all this.* Nothing would give me greater pleasure than to strike out swinging in all the concerns and claims and warnings and appeals I have voiced in all these pages.

But I'm afraid I am right. The millions of words I have read to research the hunger problem, and the millions of miles I have traveled to fight it, combine to convince me.

And I hear again that Voice I respect above all others. It tells me—He tells me—that "there will be famines and earthquakes."

3. Make the nutritional needs of your own family a matter of specific concern. (If you are a family of one, those words still apply. In fact, if you are a "family of one" in the U.S.A., you face a special problem in view of your country's tax structure and price spiral.)

Your local library, your nearby health food store, that neighbor who is a "nut on nutrition": talk, study, listen!

Take a long look at the possibility of a little garden of your own. Exactly what you do and whether or not this is economically feasible depend in large measure on the region in which you live, the growing seasons and other climatological factors, as well as the disparate context of your own lot and life style.

But do make this a subject of specific interest and action. Don't be part of the world's nutrition/hunger problem; be part of the *solution!*

4. Extend your concern for your own family to the needy of your own community. Salem Kirban, in his thought-provoking *I Predict,* says: "Widespread famine will occur even in the United States. Riots because of hunger will become unmanageable."

If that seems farfetched, even after the multitude of similar quotations I have aimed at you in the course of this study, at least listen again to the Voice you should heed when you turn off all others: *"You feed them."*

5. Support church and civic outreach to the hungry, in your own country and around the world. Of all the areas of ecological concern—the legitimate worries about the energy crisis and noise pollution and population density psychosis—remember that nothing is of more basic importance than the hunger/nutrition crisis, today and tomorrow and as time runs out.

Let me tell you how one person faced up to this problem. Or rather, how one person was *forced* to face it. But let Colin Morris tell his own story, in his own words from his *Include Me Out!* It happens that he is a clergyman, a British Methodist missionary, so his reactions to flesh-and-blood hunger are expressed within that framework. You and I too must react to hunger-which-touches-us in the world in which we live. When it does, God give us something of this man's blunt and ruthless self-appraisal.

I suspect that Morris could be classed as a theological liberal, and probably that wouldn't bother him a bit—but that really doesn't make any difference right here. I confess that I alternately wept, got angry (at myself, mostly) and nodded in 100 percent agreement as I read words like these:

Page 7: "The other day a Zambian dropped dead not a hundred yards from my front door. The pathologist said he'd died of hunger. In his shrunken stomach were a few leaves and what appeared to be a ball of grass. And nothing else."

Page 39: "I seem to have strayed a long way from the little man with the shrunken belly who started all this. But I have not forgotten him, nor ever could.

96

As a statistic he is eminently forgettable. As a fiery visitation from God he has limitless capacity to stab the conscience awake."

Further on, page 39: "Two thousand years of Christian history were blown away by the faint sigh of that little man's last breath. . . . He died without knowing that Jesus cared for him, not in a sentimental, spiritualized way, but by the offer of a square meal."

Page 40: "So God's chosen one visited the Church. He came attired not in the splendour of an Archbishop's robes or the well-cut suit of a Nonconformist prince, but in a pair of shorts and a ragged shirt, and his sceptre was an empty Biro pen."

Page 41: "He came and found the church empty. Full of people and activity and plans. But empty for him. For we did not see him. And we did not see him for his name is "legion," for there are many like him.

"He came and passed on. He walked out through the paper walls of the Church and it is too late to call him back and offer him the chief seat at the feast. So we are left with the debris of a banquet and no guest of honour."

And then the climax of this particular line of thought, also on page 41: "When our churches have rotted and our vestments have crumpled and the wind blows through the ruins of our ecclesiastical structures, all that will stand and have eternal significance are creative acts of compassion. . . ."

Of course this is not to denigrate the so-called "spiritual" ministries of the church. (I put quotation marks around that word "spiritual," because it is my firm opinion that feeding the hungry and caring for the sick *are* "spiritual" acts when done as an expression of God's love reaching out to the whole man.) I do Colin Morris something of an injustice when I quote him like this, particularly when I just lump together the above quotations. In the skilled movements of his pen they form a delicate thread, appearing again and again to tie his thoughts together in effective continuity.

My whole point in quoting him this extensively, again, is just to show the impact on this man and the influence on his thinking after that fateful moment when "a Zambian dropped dead not a hundred yards" from his front door.

In directing that you should support various activities to help the hungry (point 5, above), I mentioned the church. Let's take a few moments to look at what I regard as the very specific responsibilities a *church* (whatever its denominational label) assumes when it sets out to be a "New Testament church in faith and practice."

Listen in as Paul talks to the church in Corinth: "Now here are the directions about the money you are collecting to send to the Christians in Jerusalem" (1 Cor. 16:1).

"Now I want to tell you what God in his grace has done for the churches in Macedonia. Though they have been going through much trouble and hard times, they have mixed their wonderful joy with their deep poverty, and the result has been an overflow of giving to others. They gave not only what they could afford, but far more; and I can testify that

98

they did it because they wanted to, and not because of nagging on my part" (2 Cor. 8:1–3).

"So you also should share with those in need" (2 Cor. 8:15).

In his thoroughly readable and solidly practical *A Turned-On Church in an Uptight World,* C. Peter Wagner comments about these verses and others in the same context: "Having been oriented to contemporary church economics, I used to read these passages with the erroneous idea that they referred to some principles that churches should adopt to finance themselves."

Now note how Wagner develops his point: "I wasn't alone in this mistake. Not one of the collection of commentaries I have on First Corinthians develops this passage in the context of social service. The inference is that the offerings Paul speaks of were for the church itself. Commentators recognize the fact that Paul referred to the collection for the poor at Jerusalem, but most sermons on these texts have not attempted to arouse a sense of responsibility for the poor of our own day, but rather to increase the amount of money in the offering plates."

And then he wraps it up, to me most convincingly: "For the Corinthians this could not have been the purpose at all. The Corinthian church had few, if any, financial needs as a church organization. It met in the house of one of the members, so there was no rent, taxes, or maintenance cost. The modern idea of a fulltime, fully supported pastor had not been thought of, so they had no pastor's salary, telephone bill, or automobile expense to be concerned about. There were no Sunday School materials, no hymnals, and no church bus. . . . Paul's appeals to the Corinthians for funds had nothing to do with expenses at Corinth. It was for Jerusalem; not for the Jerusalem church expenses, but rather to help the poor people there in a material way. This is a major biblical principle: *giving on the part of Christians should be basically for others."*

I'm glad that Wagner brought it around to that word: "Christians." He reminds us that the church, after all, is people. It consists of individuals.

Does that have a familiar ring? We talked some chapters back about how hungry Planet Earth comprises individuals; how the massive dimensions of need are best understood when they are reduced to the focus of one starving child, one desperate mother or father.

Well, in the same way: *the need of those individuals can only be met through the HELP of individuals.*

So that comes back to you. Come to think of it, that also brings it back to me.

And here we are, back at the question with which we launched this chapter: "What do you want us to do?" I put that question to you, and now you can turn it right back on me.

Do we perhaps look at each other in dismay to say, "Am I supposed to give it *all* away?" Well, in a sense that is pretty drastic, but it's really a pretty good summary of the scriptural teaching.

Why *not* give it all away? That is, why not give it all to God in the sense of admitting that it is first of all His. "Not how much of my money should I give to God. Rather, how much of God's money should I keep for myself?"

Of course you have debts to pay, responsibilities to yourself, obligations to your family and to others. This same Book of books tells us that the one who doesn't take care of his family is "worse than the heathen," and illustrates the need for a sound savings program by citing the case of the ants "who labor hard all summer, gathering food for the winter."

But we are also given a very wise prayer-pattern: "Give me neither poverty or riches! Give me just enough to satisfy my needs! For if I grow rich, I may become content without God. And if I am too poor, I may steal, and thus insult God's holy name" (Prov. 30:8,9).

Sound a little radical? Think it through another step with these New Testament verses, the words of Paul to young Timothy: "Do you want to be truly rich? You already are if you are happy and good. After all, we didn't bring any money with us when we came into the world, and we can't carry away a single penny when we die. So we should be well satisfied without money if we have enough food and clothing" (1 Tim. 6:6-8).

I don't remember the poem in full (or where I read it, except that it was in the stewardship pamphlet of some religious organization), but I am haunted by the last line: "And all that he held in his cold, dead hand—was what he had given away!"

Or, "You can't take your money to heaven, but you *can* send it on ahead!"

And just one more: "Died, eh? He was pretty rich. How much did he leave?" I'm sure you know the answer: *"He left it all."*

Again and again I meet people who, when they

hear about my concerns and work, say something like, "I feel so *guilty* when I think of how much I have when so many have so little!"

My usual, sincere reply is this: "Don't be guilty. Be *grateful*. And then out of your gratitude do something to help someone else."

When I say that, I think of that wonderful couple who skips lunch one day each week and sends what they save to help the hungry . . . those wonderful youngsters in Oak Harbor, Washington, who sell pony rides (2¢ each!) to help needy children . . . those sharp high schoolers and collegians across Canada and the United States who go on weekend "Starvathons" (no food from Friday night until late Sunday; sponsored for each hour they fast as a practical means for helping others) . . . and that distinguished pastor-friend who challenged his people to give on Thanksgiving Day *only* if their gift represented some personal sacrifice, such as a meal they had missed.

I'll never forget how I felt that day in early 1972 as I packed to leave Bangladesh. The war there had just ended. I had hurried in to see how we could help, and now I was rushing back to contact other agencies and to seek all kinds of aid. There in Bangladesh some three million people had died, and now about thirty million were homeless and hungry. Uncounted other millions were in need.

I think I have learned to "travel light" in my years of constant movement around the world. But on this particular trip I had scheduled a number of interviews with very highly placed government leaders in various countries, so I did have some extra clothes along.

I looked down on the several shirts I had already folded; the suit and sport coat and extra pants. And then I thought suddenly of those who had left Bangladesh with only the clothing on their backs, and who now were coming back with virtually nothing but those same clothes, now tattered and torn.

My hosts on that trip were two wonderful missionaries of the Assemblies of God, Rev. and Mrs. Calvin Olson. Walking out from my room to the desk where Mrs. Olson was at work, I said: "Marian, I know this may seem very strange. I'm sure there aren't many Bengalis my size and shape. But ten million people left here with only the clothes on their backs, and my heart won't let me do anything else. At least they can tear up the clothing and use the cloth."

Mrs. Olson hesitated for a moment—but only for a moment. I suspect her immediate reaction had been one of practicality, to point out that my gift would be limited in its use. But then she just nodded in gentle, understanding agreement. Marian and her dear husband are one of the most Christlike missionary couples I have met anywhere in the world, and I know that her loving heart had quickly moved beyond the obvious to see what this would mean to *me*, quite apart from its value to anyone else.

So I left Bangladesh that day with an empty suitcase and a full heart.

And perhaps through the one-way glass Up There, Paul nudged Timothy and said, "See the man down there in Dacca, getting on the plane with that big smile on his face? That's what I was talking about, Tim. He's truly rich!"

And he was.

11

"They Die
One at a Time . . .

But Jesus said, "YOU feed them." (Mark 6:37)

I was driving down a busy California freeway when the answer came. For weeks I had been wrestling with the conviction that I should get deeply, personally involved in the problem of a hungry world.

For many years previously, for many millions of miles, I had been looking into the suffering face of hunger all over the world. Through all those same years and for many years before, I had been reading a Book-more-than-a-book which in simple, unmistakable words spelled out my personal responsibilities to my hungry neighbor, whoever and wherever he happened to be in this shrinking world.

I don't know how you are or what you do, but I often just talk with God as I drive along alone. So I did that now, and the question welled up naturally out of a troubled heart: "But, Father—12,000 a day. Twelve thousand every day who starve to death. That's so many, and—and I'm not an organization. I'm just one person."

And then the answer came. I suppose it was only audible to the ears of my heart, but I heard it—as clearly and unmistakably as any voice I have ever

106

A boy faces an uncertain world.

heard: "But they die one at a time, my son, *they die one at a time.*"

Have *you* felt overwhelmed by the magnitude of the world hunger/nutrition crisis as together we have examined it in these pages? Then remember: they die one at a time. So we go to help them, one at a time.

I know that's a very personal disclosure which I have made in the paragraphs above. But I want to take you even deeper into my own heart and concerns, and perhaps you will see why I feel so very deeply about this problem we have studied together.

Now let me take you back to a few months before the incident described above. On this earlier occasion, I was in Japan, en route home from troubled Laos, Cambodia and Vietnam. Everywhere I had gone I had seen the heartbreak of hunger. I had watched children succumbing to ordinary "childhood diseases" (measles, for example) because they were so weakened by longtime malnutrition: I had seen the hungry refugees who fled before the cruel face of war.

Here I was temporarily stranded in Japan, with a full day's wait before my flight home to the United States. I had checked into the airport hotel at Tokyo's great Haneda Airport, planning to dictate reports and correspondence related to my trip.

But the growing burden for a hungry world kept thrusting itself into my thoughts, interrupting my concentration, demanding my attention. For a time I put my work aside and tried to read my Bible, but there too I found my thoughts confused. So I laid my Bible down and fell to my knees in prayer.

Let me tell you, frankly, that at first that didn't

seem to help much either! About all I could do in my prayer was admit to God that the great overwhelming burden for a hungry world—which so long and so slowly had been forming in my heart and mind—had now suddenly crystallized into something specific, sharp, prodding.

But I didn't know what to do.

I seated myself at the little desk again, preparing to resume my work. First I reached out and pulled toward me the Bible which I had left there open-faced when I stopped in my reading. As I began to read at the very point where I had left off, the words seemed to reach out and grip me with paralyzing strength:

"And one of them . . . stood up . . . to predict by the Spirit that a great famine was coming"!

Now I realize that it might seem to many to be the height of presumption for anyone to "put himself" into a Bible verse such as that. I am of course aware of the specific context of this verse, dealing with a famine which was to come upon the land of Israel (and one which, incidentally, was fulfilled during the reign of Claudius).

But let me simply tell you what I did. Again I put the Bible aside and went to my knees once more, this time to pray: "Here am I, Lord, send *me*."

Of course I didn't know all that this prayer would mean. I did know, as I prayed, that someday I would have to write this book. I am sure I *didn't* know then that it would mean a change in my life's work—leaving an organization with which I was very happily engaged, to move out alone into the vast and frightening stretches of the World of Hunger.

Yet I did know there was something I had to do: to predict that a great famine was coming.

It is, you know.

I am utterly convinced of this. Three full years have passed since I rose from my knees that day, and I am more deeply, sadly convinced than ever that the hunger/crisis is here and the hunger/tragedy just ahead.

Since that prayer—since I went out to run across the world and ring my little bell and shout "The famines are coming!" to everyone who would listen—I have seen the problem come into new and sharp and dramatic focus.

Those years have seen the collapse of the "green revolution" . . . the sixty million hungry refugees of Bangladesh . . . the nightmare of Managua . . . the swiftly changing dimension of life in the western world, with suddenly dwindling resources and rocketing prices . . . the massive famine areas of India and Africa's Sahelian desert . . . the shrinking grain resources of giant nations such as the U.S.A. and the U.S.S.R.

At least 13,140,000 have starved to death since I prayed that prayer three years ago. God only knows how many others have died as a result of longtime malnutrition. That figure is probably too astronomical for any of us to comprehend.

The world has 200 million more people now than it had the day that I prayed in Japan; and you know and I know that we have not begun to increase our food production to care for them.

Now, a third time I invite you to come deep, deep down into the concerns of my heart.

110

Several times in these pages I have quoted for you the prediction of my Lord and Saviour: "And there will be famines and earthquakes."

But have you really stopped to think what that means? Those words are from the Gospel of St. Matthew, chapter 24, and they are in an incredible context. Jesus Christ is telling about the last days. He predicts the famines and the earthquakes as "the beginning of the horrors to come," and then he delineates some of those horrors in more than living color.

But at last you'll find it, in verse 30: *"And the nations of the world will see me arrive in the clouds of heaven, with power and great glory."*

Do you know what I hear as I read that majestic promise? Welling up in my heart are the triumphant strains of that great song, "The King Is Coming!"

Now, finally, with that in mind, picture this scene: "But when I, the Messiah, shall come in my glory, and all the angels with me, then I shall sit upon my throne of glory. And all the nations shall be gathered before me" (Matt. 25:31,32).

Here we are, the nations of earth, gathered before the King of the Universe, the Ruler of Eternity. Quiet now. He begins to speak!

How quickly we hush. For all these centuries we have waited to hear His voice. At last He is here, and we wait to hear His first great proclamation.

We listen, and He says: "Thank you."

Just that. So simply. "Thank you."

We look at Him open-mouthed and uncomprehending, and He explains: "Thank you. You see—while I was gone, I was hungry and you fed Me; I was thirsty and you gave Me water; I was a stranger

111

and you invited Me into your homes; naked and you clothed Me; sick and in prison, and you visited Me."

We listen, but still we do not fully understand: "Lord, when did we do those things?"

And then He tells us, and our hearts begin to know and understand: *"When you did it to these my brothers, you were doing it to Me."*

I see. Now I see!

That was His brother there in Laos. Oh, I'm so glad I could hold out that can of food.

That was His little brother, there in Cambodia. I'm glad I could at least hold him in my arms and ease his pain a bit, before he died.

That was His elderly brother there, sitting in confusion in the ruins of Managua. Thank God You helped me help him, just a little.

But—that's His brother, holding out that thin and pleading hand in India.

That's His brother, crawling across the sun-drenched desert in Upper Volta, pleading with parched lips for just a drink of water.

That's His brother, there in Haiti, with his black face caked with dust and his tiny baby in his arms, and his eyes are eloquent in their silent pleading as we meet him on the mountain trail.

Friend, the time is short.

The King is coming.

His brothers are out there, waiting.

I'll go help them.

I want to hear Him say it when He comes: "Thank you."

What about you?

"Jesus said, *'You* feed them.' "

12

"Update"—
An Open Letter

"When will this happen?" the disciples asked him later. . . . "What events will signal your return, and the end of the world?" (Matthew 24:3, TLB)

Six years have gone by since the preceding pages were written.

Millions of words have been written about the world's hunger problems since then—and millions of people have starved to death.

I myself have traveled another million-or-more miles to help the hungry; the organization which I head, Food for the Hungry International, has shipped additional millions of pounds of food and has expended millions of dollars (given by people like *you*, people who care) in an effort to help.

In the foregoing pages I have described some of the hurt and hunger and heartbreak of Africa. My heart sank a few days ago when I read the flat statement of the Director General of the FAO (Food and Agriculture Organization of the United Nations) that Africa is at least ten percent worse off today than it was ten years ago.

What has happened? Where do we go from here?

Let me summarize some of the things which happened in the closing days of the 1970s.

Disaster

The natural disasters continue to happen. One of the most devastating was Guatemala—but this was followed by floods in Mexico, hurricanes in the Carribean (especially in the Dominican Republic), and by other devastating earthquakes in Iran and Romania.

The world situation has been aggravated by sudden new refugee movements of incredible proportions. One friend said to me: "Thank God that He has held back the natural disasters a bit in the past four years. There is no way in which all of the various relief organizations, already taxed beyond their ability to help by the mammoth size of the refugee problem, could have geared up to face another Guatemala."

But the disasters will continue to come, and we must stand ready to help. As we do, we find encouragement again in those words of Isaiah 58:11: "If thou draw out thy soul to the hungry . . . *the Lord shall guide thee continually" (KJV).*

We have seen it. And we expect to see it again.

Let me give you an illustration. On January 19, 1976, I met in Guatemala City with the disaster relief coordinators for that country. With me were Dr. Dean Flora, our Latin America Director, the Reverend Isai Calderon of the Church of God, and my wife Lorraine.

I put to the disaster relief coordinators what I felt was an obvious question: "What plan do you have against the threat of a major earthquake, or volcanic eruption?"

115

I remember how they looked at each other, smiled, and then said to us (almost gently and condescendingly): "We don't have earthquakes in Guatemala. Not since 1916 or 1917 have we had an earthquake."

No earthquakes in Guatemala? Three weeks later, to the very day, Guatemala was ripped by one of the most devastating earthquakes in human history. More than 20,000 people died; over a million people were left homeless; the economy has not yet fully begun to recover.

But, thank God, they *did* have a plan. Admittedly it was skeletal, preliminary—put it was a plan.

And, more importantly, God Himself had a plan. We ourselves, on the very day of that meeting, asked Isai Calderon if he would serve as our volunteer director at Guatemala. I called my office in the United States, and asked that food be shipped to Guatemala immediately. It was—75,624 pounds of food. No, we didn't really know that an earthquake would come so soon. But by the goodness of God, that food arrived the day *before* the earthquake. So when we ourselves returned, within thirty-six hours of the earthquake, we were "off and running" with what in the weeks which followed became a major assistance program.

And there were other beautiful indications of God's own interest. During those three weeks between our meeting and the earthquake I had appeared on TV's "700 Club" with our beloved friend Dr. Pat Robertson. The TV taping was done the day *before* the earthquake; when the program was shown across the United States, it came just at the time when the whole world was focusing attention on Guatemala. The "700 Club" assisted us and other agencies most generously, and inspired others to help. The result was one of the greatest outpourings of love the world has ever seen.

In a disaster, one of the important things is to get there as quickly as possible. I shall never forget that day in Bucharest, right after the Romanian earthquake, when I met with the faculty and students of the Baptist seminary there. Their buildings had been severely damaged, and would have to be torn down and replaced. But the Romanian Christians were in good spirits as we talked. In the back of the little circle with whom I was talking stood the wife of the president. I noticed that her eyes were full of tears, and so I paused, waiting to see what she wanted to say.

I was deeply moved by her words: "Oh, Sir, it is not only that you came. You came so *quickly*."

May God always make that true. I have not said much in these preceding pages about Food for the Hungry itself, but I want you to know that we will always stand ready, as God enables, to help when the hurricanes and floods and cyclones and tidal waves and earthquakes strike.

You see, there *will* be earthquakes.

Famine

And there will also be famines. He said it, you remember. The Lord Jesus Christ. He said, "The nations and kingdoms of the earth will rise against each other, and there will be famines and earthquakes in many places" (Matthew 24:7, *TLB*).

As the natural disasters have continued, the famines have also grown worse throughout the world, particularly in Africa.

On September 1, 1980, *U.S. News and World Report* summed it up most succinctly:

"Not since famine struck the Sahel region of

West Africa seven years ago, claiming 250,000 lives, has the continent faced so grave a danger . . . Experts estimated that as many as 60 million people are endangered. . . .

Drought has cast a swath of devastation from the Red Sea to the black tribal lands of South Africa, leaving in its wake parched fields, decimated livestock herds and uncounted dead."

Refugees

The disaster and famine conditions in the world were complicated further by the movement of multiplied millions of people. First refugees from Indochina fled to the United States, and a huge wave then moved westward to Thailand. This wave continued, and then spread out, particularly the Vietnamese refugee "boat people," to Malaysia and Hong Kong and Indonesia and the Philippines and Singapore.

In 1980, after Russian troops rolled into Afghanistan, hundreds of thousands of Afghan refugees fled to Pakistan.

Meanwhile, as fighting raged in Ethiopia, hundreds of thousands of refugees fled in all directions in East Africa. Somalia, for example, had over 1.4 million refugees as 1981 dawned.

Along with the major relief/development agencies, we of Food for the Hungry found ourselves caught up in massive relief activities in all of these places. For example, we began our refugee activities in Thailand in May, 1975, just after the first forty refugees had arrived from Vietnam. Somehow, our hearts told us that they would be followed by many, many thousands of others.

Since then, it has been our privilege to offer major

assistance in Thailand, feeding up to as many as 30,000 every day and helping the refugees assist themselves with poultry and piggery projects.

Late in 1975, we had begun a tireless program of trying to find large-scale resettlement opportunities for the refugees in under-developed areas of South America particularly.

Earlier that year, from May 1975 to October, we had operated the unique "Hope Village" facility, the only one of its kind in the United States, offering education, job placement help and general orientation to American life for over 1,000 Vietnamese refugees whom I personally had sponsored out of Vietnam.

But always our hearts were haunted by what we knew about the boat people. In the last days of South Vietnam, in April, 1975, I had had the dubious distinction of putting the first of the boat people into the water. (A "dubious" distinction because that particular boat did not make it. It was taken illegally by certain elements in the South Vietnamese police, and the people on board were captured and held for ransom). I myself spent my last days in Vietnam (in a country I had known and loved for many years) hiding out from those same crooked elements of the police. But God enabled me finally to leave, and to share with two beloved friends (Dr. Garth Hunt of Living Bibles International, and Ha Jimmy, a dedicated young Vietnamese Montagnard), the great privilege of sponsoring over 1,800 Vietnamese refugees in their escape from Vietnam and their new life in the United States.

But, through 1976 and 1977, that burden persisted. Other little boats kept coming, first in a trickle and then in a giant wave. We were haunted by the realization that at least 40 percent of those who set out in the rugged waters

119

of the South China Sea, trusting their lives to those pathetical tiny little boats, did not make it. They died terrible deaths at sea because of thirst or hunger or dehydration, or when their little boats capsized, or at the hands of the pirates who incredibly still infest those waters.

As these words are written, the "boat people" are no longer in the headlines. They had a brief day of media attention in mid-1979, and then the newspeople turned their attention elsewhere.

The boat people aren't now in the headlines. But as these words are written, they *are* still in the water. And so we are still out there too, with our rescue ship still combing the seas, trying to help. We had begun preparations to launch such a ship in 1976. We are not a large organization, and it took us a long time to amass the resources and buy a former Australian naval vessel. Finally, in late 1978, we went to sea to help.

And as I look at the record of the hundreds and hundreds of people whom we have been privileged to rescue at sea, I remember my own experience of standing on the deck of that ship with the binoculars, praying as my eyes searched the waters. I will always regard it as one of the greatest privileges God has ever given us.

Let me recite for you one such experience. In a publication of Food for the Hungry, I described it like this:

> It was a day I'll never forget: standing on the deck of our rescue ship, *SS Akuna,* as we looked into the faces of 116 tearfully grateful Vietnamese boat people.
>
> We have been privileged to save hundreds of lives during these last eighteen months of rescue operations, but we have never encountered a warmer or obviously more grateful group than

this. After Ha Jimmy and I had finished talking to them, one of them stood up to say something like this: "We wish we had something to give you. But we left everything behind in Vietnam— and what little we had was taken away from us by the pirates. But we do want you to have this . . ." and he held out the compass from their little boat.

I don't know when I have ever been more deeply moved. Here was the thing, humanly speaking, which had led them to us and thus saved their lives. When I recovered my composure, I said: "I feel like another pirate to take your compass. But you will not need it now, for you are safe here on the deck of our ship!"

And then I added: "Ha Jimmy and I have just given you another and more important Compass—the Bible, the Word of God. You will need this special Compass, as you begin your new life in America or some other part of the world. There will be problems there—problems of adjustment, problems when people do not understand you.

"Follow this Compass, the Bible! Let it lead you straight to God. Just as your compass brought you to safety on our ship, so this Compass, the Bible, can lead you to the new life found only in God through belief in Jesus Christ, His Only Son."

But a Ray of Hope . . .

Admittedly, as we look at the prospect of more famines and earthquakes, and the continuing complexity of the refugee problems, it's a dark picture. But there are rays of hope.

Global 2000 Report to the President, in the United States, made this statement: "Many nations around the world are now taking new approaches—replanting deforested areas, conserving energy, making family planning measures available, using natural predators and selective pesticides to protect crops instead of broadscale destructive application of chemicals."

Millions of people, particularly in the United States but also in Australia, Canada and Europe, are taking a new look at life-style. Admittedly, just eating less at home does not directly contribute to meeting the famine and disaster needs around the world. But it is an expression of one's sense of his individual responsibility—and an indication that we do recognize that our planet must conserve its resources if we are to survive.

We at Food for the Hungry are especially encouraged because of the opportunities that we see to help people to help themselves through the practical utilization of the free basics with which God has endowed Planet Earth.

Let me explain that. Over against everything I have said in all the preceding pages, I must state my deep conviction that God is not caught by surprise by the desperate plight of our world. He has already endowed the planet with all that it will ever need to sustain all of the population it will ever experience. The problem is that we have been poor stewards. Perhaps you will forgive me if I say, "lousy stewards," to use a very American expression.

I think it was my good friend and associate, Dr. Dean Nauman, who first helped me to see how we can utilize those three basics—the sun, the wind, the rain—to help people help themselves.

Dean is a philosopher, a theologian. His doctorate is in education. But he is a very practical "hands on" person—and also a deeply committed Christian who knows that God ultimately has the answers.

As our Director of Agri-Research in Food for the Hungry, Dean has developed practical tools to help people help themselves: solar cookers and grain dryers, to use the free resource of the sun . . . simple and preliminary experiments (which will be continued and expanded) to utilize wind energy . . . and particularly tools for hydroponic (soil-less) growing, which will have particular application in the crowded urban areas and also in the arid zones of earth. Meanwhile, we have been involved in major projects of simple water resource development in places such as Haiti, Kenya, Guatemala and Peru.

I like these projects! You see, people must learn that they can use the sun to cook their food and dry their grain; that they can harness the wind for low-cost alternative energy; that they can trap the rain, and have water for their own needs and for their animals for perhaps two years from a single rainfall in Africa. And they must learn that, even though they stand on barren earth as that of the northwest peninsula of Haiti, they really don't need it, for they can have a "garden in a box" through the three-centuries-old techniques of hydroponics.

These approaches are good because they not only help people to help themselves, without the expensive application of modern computerized techniques of agri-business which are beyond the understanding and the reach of most of the people of the world, but also point people to the God who causes the sun to shine and the wind to blow and the rain to fall. "The Lord of Hosts is a wonderful teacher and gives the farmer wisdom" (Isaiah 28:29, *TLB*).

Looking Ahead

And we need all these things.

The other day, in a TV interview, I held my precious one-year-old granddaughter, Melissa, in my arms before the cameras. Even as we were filming, I thought suddenly of the plight of the needy children of the world. Here was my healthy granddaughter, a wonderful gift of God.

But out there, millions and millions of children in the world are dying because they don't have enough food to eat or to keep them alive and well.

If Melissa lives to be 50 years old, she will live in an incredible world of *ten billion people*—two and a half times as many people as now. And nine out of ten will live in the famine area.

Right now, the current estimate is that at least 3 million people die each year of starvation or of malnutrition-caused diseases.

That now figures out to 27,400 a day.

In other words, look at your watch. *In the next 30 minutes, another 600 people will have died*—because they don't have enough food to keep them alive and well.

That's almost overwhelming. But I still cling to that one thought. "They die one at a time . . . so we can *help them* one at a time."

And we must.

Footnotes

1. *U.S. News & World Report,* Dec. 6, 1972.
2. *U.S. News & World Report,* Nov. 9, 1970, p. 29.
3. Arthur McCormick, *The Population Problem* (New York: Crowell, 1970), p. 6.
4. *Scientific American,* March 1956.
5. Colin Morris, *Include Me Out* (London: Epworth Press, 1968), p. 43.
6. William and Paul Paddock, *Famine—1975!* (Boston: Little, Brown & Co., 1967).
7. *South China Post,* Hong Kong.
8. *The Protein Gap,* Bureau of Technical Assistance of AID, p. 2.
9. Paul and Anne Ehrlich, *Population Resources Environment* (San Francisco: Freeman, 1970), p. 76.
10. Paddock, *Famine—1975!,* pp. 64,65.
11. *Newsweek,* June 4, 1973.
12. Paddock, *Famine—1975!,* pp. 56,57.
13. Gordon Bridger and Maurice de Soissons, *Famine in Retreat* (London: Dent & Sons, 1970).
14. *Haiti—Politics of Squalor* (Boston: Houghton Mifflin, 1971), p. 25.
15. *Earthquakes,* Nelson Doubleday, Inc., pp. 3,4.
16. Sherwood Eliot Wirt, *The Social Conscience of the Evangelical* (New York: Harper & Row, 1968), p. 39.

Bibliography

Bibliography

World Population

Allison, Anthony, ed. *Population Control.* Middlesex, Eng.: Penguin, 1970.

Ehrlich, Paul R. *The Population Bomb.* New York: Ballantine, 1968.

Ehrlich, Paul R., and Ehrlich, Anne H. *Population Resources Environment.* San Francisco: Freeman, 1970.

Malthus, Thomas Robert. (Edited and introduced by Gertrude Himmelfarb.) *On Population.* New York: Random House, 1960.

McCormick, Arthur. *The Population Problem.* New York: Crowell, 1970.

Ng, L.K.Y., and Mudd, S., eds. *The Population Crisis, Implications, and Plans for Action.* Indianapolis: Indiana University Press, 1965.

World Hunger Problem

Borgstrom, Georg. *The Hungry Planet*. New York: Collier, 1965.

Bridger, Gordon, and Soissons, Maurice de. *Famine in Retreat*. London: Dent & Sons, 1970.

Castro, Josue de. *The Black Book of Hunger*. Boston: Beacon Press, 1967.

Hardin, Clifford M., ed. *Overcoming World Hunger*. London: Prentice-Hall, 1969.

Hopcraft, Arthur. *Born To Hunger*. London: Heinemann, 1968.

Leinwand, Gerald, general editor. *Hunger*. New York: Simon & Schuster, 1971.

Paddock, William, and Paddock, Paul. *Famine—1975!* Boston: Little, Brown & Co., 1967.

Segal, Ronald. *The Anguish of India*. New York: New American Library, 1965.

Poverty in America

Bagdikian, Ben H. *In the Midst of Plenty*. New York: New American Library, 1964.

Christian Social Responsibility

Gollwitzer, Helmut (trans. by David Cairns). *The Rich Christians and Poor Lazarus*. New York: Macmillan, 1970.

Moberg, David O. *Inasmuch—Christian Social Responsibility in the Twentieth Century*. Grand Rapids: Eerdmans, 1968.

Morris, Colin. *Include Me Out! Confessions of an Ecclesiastical Coward*. London: Epworth Press, 1968.

Simon, Paul. *A Hungry World* (Christian Encounter Series). St. Louis: Concordia, 1966.

Wagner, C. Peter. *A Turned-On Church in an Uptight World.* Grand Rapids: Zondervan, 1971.

Wirt, Sherwood Eliot. *The Social Conscience of the Evangelical.* New York: Harper & Row, 1968.

Ecological, Prophetic, General

Johnson, Huey D., ed. *No Deposit—No Return.* Reading, Mass.: Addison-Wesley Publishing Co., 1970.

Kik, J. Marcellus. *Matthew Twenty-Four.* Swengal, PA.: Herendeen, 1948.

King, Maurice, ed. *Medical Care in Developing Countries. (A Primer on the Medicine of Poverty and A Symposium from Makerere.)* Nairobi: Oxford University Press, 1966.

Lindsey, Hal, with Carlson, C.C. *The Late Great Planet Earth.* Grand Rapids: Zondervan, 1970.

Osborn, Fairfield. *Our Plundered Planet.* Boston: Little, Brown & Co., 1948.

Stedman, Ray C. *What on Earth's Going to Happen?* Glendale, CA: Regal, 1970.

Toffler, Alvin. *Future Shock.* New York: Random House, 1970.

Vassiliev, M., and Gouschev, S., eds. *Life in the Twenty-First Century.* (First published in Russia in 1959.) Middlesex, Eng.: Penguin, 1961.